THE BUSINESS

EVERYTHING YOU NEED TO KNOW ABOUT THE HOLLYWOOD DANCE INDUSTRY OF **DANCE**

By Courtney Miller Jr. and Tim Stevenson

LEARN | BOOK | SUCCEED

This book is dedicated to our family, friends, and dance teachers who have inspired us over the years.

ACKNOWLEDGEMENTS:

Tim Stevenson

I would like to acknowledge some people who have helped support and provide insight to this book. I would like to thank my family who has been there for me through every venture I have ever chosen to take on in my life. Thank you, Mom for all your prayers you send my way. Thank you to my sisters, Miriam and Tenesia for always inspiring me.

I would like to thank the people who always stimulate my entrepreneurial mind - thank you Miguel Tejeda, Courtney Miller Jr. and Tyson Garner. Thank you to the ones who are always looking out for my best interests, so thank you Ross Mulholland, Karen Fujimoto, and Eddie Garcia.

A very special thanks goes to Jessica Livoti-Morales for her patience during the editing process; we could not have done it without you!

I am so blessed to have had a career in dance that has lead up to this book. I know the value and fulfillment that comes from sharing experiences with each other - this book is a step toward that goal.

ACKNOWLEDGEMENTS:

Courtney Miller Jr.

My journey through this business would not be possible without the help, inspiration, and guidance of the many people whom I have been blessed to know. First, is my mother, Lanita, who saw the potential in me early on. Next, my sisters, Shalana and Rashona, "The Twins", and my little brother, Chris. I am continually inspired by the creativity of my two children, Tommy and Jaira, I love you both very much!

I would also like to thank the dance teachers who have influenced my dance and choreographic careers. Michelle Johnston (Bebe from "A Chorus Line"), Michelle Simmons ("Thriller"), Ka-Ron Brown (Los Angeles County High School for the Arts), Phineas Newborn III (" Breakin"), and Matthew Rushing (Alvin Ailey).

A special thanks also goes out to the choreographers who helped me along the way in my career. Doriana Sanchez & Bubba Carr (Desi Awards), Jamie King (Carmen Electra and Prince), Frank Gatson (En Vogue, Destiny's Child), and, finally, Travis Payne, and Lavelle Smith (Michael Jackson).

A special thanks goes to my close friends, Brian Carter, Eric Seats, Marce Sellier, Claudia Gonzalez, Paul Kim, David Kater, Vanessa Hidalgo, my friends for life!

And finally, a huge THANK YOU (Jessica, I promise not to use all caps again.) to two important people responsible for the creation of this book. Jessica Livoti-Morales, for your amazing job editing and re-editing this book, and Tim Stevenson, the Co-Author of this book,. Thank you for your creativity, your entrepreneurial spirit, and your wisdom during this process.

Bios

Bio - Courtney Miller Jr.

I grew up in Gardena, California in a lower middle class neighborhood with a mixture of motels, apartments, and houses. My mother always believed that too much free time on a child's hands would lead to trouble, so I did everything from playing the trombone and accordion, to acting. But I fell in love with dance, and there was one person to blame for that: Michael Jackson.

MTV was new back then. We had recently purchased cable television and all MTV would feature were rock groups. That changed when Michael performed the "Thriller" music video. MTV marketed the video as a world premiere, something new at that time, and my sisters, mother and I sat on the fold-out couch in the living room and watched "Thriller" and the "Making Of" behind-the-scenes video. I loved the video, but what hooked me was the behind-the-scenes work that choreographer Michael Peters put Michael and the dancers through. That behind the scenes video still resonates with me today.

It was after watching "Thriller" that I started dancing around the house. I was Michael, and I made my twin sisters be the zombies. We recorded the music video on VHS, watched it over and over again facing the television, and committed every step to memory. Of course, the fact that we learned the video facing the television meant that we learned the whole thing backwards. But we knew all the steps, so it didn't matter to us. My mother was so proud, and did not hesitate to call neighbors over to watch her kids dance. But I wasn't used to performing in front of others, and truth be told, I felt that her gloating over her kids was sort of like bragging, and I hated bragging. She would gather an eager audience ready to watch her "babies" perform. I would explain that I didn't want to dance for a crowd. She would threaten that I would immediately have to wash the sink full of dishes if I didn't, and so, crying, I would perform "Thriller" with those famous shoulder shrugs.

"Thriller" was just the beginning. My sisters and I caught the performing bug, and we would choreograph routines to music by MC Hammer, New Edition, and other up-and-coming stars of the day.

Thus, a choreographer was born. I was 15. I choreographed a new routine every week from the ages of 15-17. I loved the music of that time, and I felt inspired. Due to the Cosby Show, (especially the episodes where the kids would lip sync and perform for the family) my sisters and I performed for our immediate and extended family quite often. That provided me the experience I needed to audition and perform with confidence later in life.

At 15, I decided to audition for the prestigious Los Angeles County High School for the Arts. I was still mainly a hip hop dancer, but I met one dancer who would forever change my perception and outlook on contemporary dance. During the audition to get into the dance department, there were only six male dancers in the room of about 50. One of the dancers, Mathew Rushing, made my mouth hit the floor. I was always of the mind-set that tights and ballet shoes were for sissies. Of course, to audition for this school, you had to do both- and perform a ballet and lyrical/contemporary routine. I quickly found out that Mathew was not there to audition, but rather, he was there to serve as an assistant to the teacher holding the audition. He was so talented that he was being used as an example of the "right" way to perform the movement. For the first time in my life, I was intimidated. He was graceful, flexible, and had amazing control. I was the complete opposite. When I jumped, I caught air, but I looked like I was swimming, especially on *jetes*. I couldn't even touch my toes and I didn't even know what half of the words spoken in French meant. After the audition, I knew that I had better look for another school option, because I was sure I wasn't going to get in. To my surprise, I got the letter inviting me to the school. Maybe it was out of pity, or maybe they needed boys, but I didn't care- I was ready to dance.

That was it! I took four hours of technique every day for the next three years in school. In addition to my technique classes at school, I took another three hours at a local studio in my neighborhood, mainly in jazz. My jazz teacher, Michelle Johnston, played BeBe in the film, "A Chorus Line." In school, I took ballet, modern, and lyrical class. After my first year, I could see huge improvements. I could do the splits, hold my leg next to my ear, and I could understand much of the ballet jargon. During the summer, I stayed busy by attending classes at UCLA with the Bella Lewitzsky's

Dance Company and I took conservatory classes at California State University, Los Angeles.

By the time I was 16 and had a little technique under my belt, I was ready to audition for a dance agent. My sisters and I auditioned with the adults for the Bobby Ball Agency, and we got our first agent, Teresa Taylor. At the age 17, Teresa, who saw my potential, sent me to every audition, even if it was out of my age range. I auditioned for Madonna's, Janet Jackson's, and Paula Abdul's choreographers while still too young to actually work on the jobs. This helped me immensely. I was too old to audition for kids' roles, but too young to be considered an adult. I used this time to network and meet the players: Choreographers, Dancers, Agents, Directors, and Producers. It served me well, because by the time I was 18, I booked work consistently.

On my 18th birthday, while I was still attending the Los Angeles County High School for the Arts, I went to an audition held by choreographers Fatima (Will Smith) and Stretch (Mariah Carey) at Alley Cat Studios in Hollywood. Along with over 300 other dancers, I auditioned for Michael Jackson's newest video "Remember the Time." I remember landing the job and working for about a week in both rehearsals and the shoot. We shot at Universal Studios and when MTV aired the "World Premiere," I was on the couch with my family (our favorite spot), VCR set to record, watching myself in the very living room where I first learned how to dance.

The following year, after graduating from high school, I auditioned for, and landed my second job with Michael: the *American Music Awards* for a song called "Dangerous". This time, I was working with Lavelle Smith, one of Michael's dancer/choreographers from the "Bad" Tour and Travis Payne (choreographer for the "This Is It!" World Tour. These two people, along with Frank Gatson (choreographer for Beyonce, Rihanna, and Usher), would play a major role in my career by offering me the opportunity to choreograph.

Travis, whom I had met as a dancer on the set of "Remember," hired me for several jobs afterward. While working on a Tevin Campbell music video, I met a big-haired Jamie King (Madonna), who also later took me under his wing. By the time we all met again, Jamie was one of Michael's back- up dancers for the "Dangerous" Tour, Travis was choreographing for Michael, and I was excited about my chances to show both of them my dance and choreographic abilities.

During rehearsal, I was placed off Michael's front left shoulder for most of the performance, the perfect place for my mother to see me. I choreographed small sections of the performance and killed the dance once we went "live". Shortly after, Travis asked me to join him and Lavelle as a choreographic team and L.T.C. choreography was born.

From 1992 –1996, we choreographed everything for Michael, including the most expensive music video ever made, "Scream", the short film *Ghosts*, and his "History" World Tour. We also worked with Brandy, Diana Ross, Guess Jeans, L'Oreal, Levi's, Paula Abdul, and many others.

While working as a choreographer with Lavelle and Travis, I would also work as a dancer for Jamie King. I danced for Carmen Electra and Prince while working with him. As politics would have it, Travis asked me to make a decision as to whether I was going to be a dancer working for Jamie or a choreographer working with L.T.C. I chose choreography, but will always have respect for what Jamie did for me then and what he is doing now.

As with many talented, collaborative groups, egos grew to the point where each member believed that they could do better all by themselves. And so, after the History Tour was over, L.T.C.-well, at least the "C" part of the group-broke up and I started working as a solo choreographer. Since that time, I have choreographed memorable performances for Britney Spears, Usher, and Destiny's Child. Now that this book is finished, I can turn my attention onto a screenplay I'm almost finished with, and a reality television show based on the inner workings of one of Los Angeles' largest dance agencies.

*U*nlike many of my peers, I did not grow up in dance studios learning movement and doing dance steps my whole life. In fact, sports played a big part in my early life. I played baseball, soccer, football, and tennis at a very competitive level. I was a varsity football player, earning awards in my league; and an Olympic development soccer player, ranked as one of the best players in the Western Hemisphere in my teens. Many of my childhood teammates have gone on to become some of the best soccer players in the world.

Dance was just something I liked to mimic from watching *Soul Train*, *American Bandstand* and being inspired by artists like, MC Hammer, Michael Jackson, Bobby Brown, New Edition, James Brown, Gene Kelly and more. I would mimic these people because I loved music and dance made me feel good. But more importantly at the time, dancing in my garage at home helped me with my coordination in the field.

It wasn't until my senior year of high school that I realized how much I really loved to perform. Every year at school, there was an annual dance concert. Two of my sports buddies decided to audition for the show, hoping to impress any cute girls who might be there. I decided to join them, and we started to put together our routine. We would practice in the school quad at night and watch the shadows cast by the reflected light to make sure we were in sync. We had no idea about dance studios, mirrors, or traditional choreography, but we knew what we liked. We all were big fans of MC Hammer and a group called Guy, so we started with that. We worked hard practicing our routine, and were proud of our "choreography"- which consisted of repeating a step at least four times until we changed to another one. When the audition day came, we threw down our routine and were an instant hit!

When show day came, we were surprised to find out that this was the first time that the dance concert had ever sold out. The entire football team, soccer team, and basketball team had bought tickets to support us. When it was time for us to perform, the screams and yells were so loud we could barely hear the music. Our routine was called "Timmy's Jam," since I was the leader of the group. I heard the crowd roar and couldn't explain the wonderful feeling I had. From that moment on, I knew I was a performer.

After the show, a woman who owned a dance studio offered us free rehearsal space in exchange for just being around to inspire other boys to dance. We took her up on her offer and went off into the dance world. In college I decided to continue investigating what dance was all about. All it took was walking past a room full of hot girls in jazz class! I immediately signed up for the course, even though I didn't know what jazz was. For the next two years, I was religiously taking jazz classes and perfecting my hip-hop skills. I was able to join a dance company called Common Ground, where I learned how to be part of a group and mastered different dance styles.

When a friend asked me if I wanted to go to LA to audition for a dance agent, I said, "Sure....what's a dance agent?" She explained to me that if I wanted to be in music videos, tours and shows, a dance agent would help me do all those things. Even though all my fellow dancers thought I was crazy, I knew what I wanted and went to the audition. Three days later, I signed with the Bobby Ball Agency in Hollywood.

But signing with an agent was only the beginning. I had big dreams and being a dancer is hard work! I went to audition after audition with no call backs. So I went on more auditions, and I got some callbacks, but I still didn't book a job for a long time. I didn't give up however; and finally, after countless auditions, I landed my first job.

The gig was working on tour with Carmen Electra, a singer who was produced by Prince. It was a huge job, which led to more auditions and jobs with Diana Ross at the Super Bowl, TLC, Queen Latifah, the Grammys, *Soul Train* Music Awards, CMT Music Awards, and the MTV Music Awards. I had the pleasure of working with great choreographers such as Barry Lather, Adam Shankman, Jamie King, Travis Payne, Tina Landon, Eddie Garcia, Lavelle Smith, Rosaro and Jamal, and more. I had accomplished all of my dreams, even though people told me that I couldn't make it in such a competitive industry. After two years, I could walk into an audition and be recognized among dancers, choreographers, and directors.

Just like that long-ago performance at the high school dance concert, I was still constantly making up my own steps and throwing them around to see what felt good. When I decided I wanted to start working as a choreographer, I put together a reel, gave it to a dance agent, and signed a contract on the spot. Though I was excited to have a choreographic agent, being a choreographer had its own set of challenges and politics I never knew existed. Whose work gets submitted for the job by the agency? Who knows who? Who has the connections to book the job?

As a way to get into choreography, I started to assist other choreographers and offered my own input on jobs. Finally, at an audition to be a dancer in a Chris Rock video, I was approached by the producer to choreograph! I landed my first choreography job. Since then, I have gone on to choreograph for Jennifer Lopez, Jo Dee Messina, Lone Star, and Shane Minor.

Besides my work as an author, dancer, and choreographer, I'm the owner of Dance Atak dance conventions and a writer/producer of music for up-and-coming artists.

T*able of Contents*

Why This Book?

*A*s two of the top dancers/choreographers in this industry, we know what it takes to make it in the Hollywood dance scene. With over 30 years experience, our advice will provide you with the staying power necessary for a long and successful career. The content of our book is not skewed by the pressure or influence of a dance agent, choreographer, producer, or a director. You are getting our unbiased opinion and true-to-life testimonials based on our personal experiences. We have worked intimately with the biggest stars in the business today. Our list of credits include Michael Jackson, Jennifer Lopez, Beyonce', Britney Spears, and Usher. So we have a keen understanding of what it takes to perform with the biggest stars. We have choreographed or performed on every award show imaginable, including MTV, American Music, The Grammys, Billboard, Country Music Television, and The Soul Train Awards, so we know what it takes to perform on the biggest stages.

But we didn't start killing it with Michael Jackson from day one. We both started from the same place as you. We've taken side jobs to make extra money during hard times. This includes dancing at *Bar mitzvahs* singing "Hava Nagila" and "YMCA". We've been there, struggling to make ends meet between jobs, just like you.

Like many dancers, we had a dream, we worked hard to perfect our craft, and it led us to choreograph and dance in music videos, world tours, and television shows.

Now that we've done this for some time, it's important for us to give back to the industry that has supported us with amazing experiences and careers. We have already had success in helping individual dancers with their careers by either directly or indirectly providing them their very first choreography and dance jobs in Hollywood. Very few dancers have those kinds of mentors to help them in the early stages of their career.

Most importantly, the reason why you should read and apply this book is because we truly care about the industry, and, by extension, your success. We care about the industry's continued growth and feel that the only way dancers will eventually be treated with the same respect as an actor or model, is by educating each individual so that they can learn, book, succeed, and grow the industry.

We don't want you to be only an amazing dancer, we want you to have a good sense of the politics of the business, be smart with your money, and we want you to look at what other opportunities dance can provide you. Upon completion of this book, you will be able to apply lessons learned into other key areas in the entertainment business including: choreography, producing, directing, writing or acting.

Reading this book is just the beginning. Attending one of our seminars will provide you with the in-depth, hands on experience and knowledge you need to overcome some unforeseen obstacles and questions. This book provides you with insight that most dancers don't get or will learn the hard way, if at all. We are your "Cliff Notes!" ......

There will be many highs and lows, but through it all, we want to be there to help you stay focused on your goals.

Good luck to you and thanks for picking up our book!

-Courtney & Tim

Why Now?

Now, more than ever before, dance is everywhere. Television shows like "So You Think You Can Dance", "America's Best Dance Crew", and "Dancing With The Stars", are on millions of televisions in millions of homes weekly. Every time you turn on the television, there is another show featuring dance. Some good, many not-so-good, but the important point to note is that many people, young and old, are starting to take major notice of dance.

With so many new opportunities, there are more dancers than ever hoping to be the next contestant on one of these shows. Many of them have no idea what to expect if they make the show, or what to do after the show ends. Many think they will have fame and fortune (Well, at least fame!) once the show airs, only to be disappointed a year later when they are contemplating what happened to all the attention they once had.

Many new dancers, who are technically amazing, have hopes of going to Hollywood, booking a job, and making money. Very soon, they find out that technique has very little to do with their ability to work. Frustrated, they return back to their home state and try to decide what's next.

This does not have to be your fate. True, there are thousands of dancers and only a few jobs. However, there are things you can do in order to increase the odds of you booking a job over the others. This book, attending our seminars, and keeping in contact with us along the way for both advice and encouragement, will help you stay on track.

The dance world has never been as competitive as it is today. For proof of that, go visit the next audition for some pop artist. You have hip-hop dancers, jazz dancers, and others all in the same room. Not too long ago, dancers could not do *both* hip-hop and jazz. Those that could do both, worked consistently. Now *everyone* can do jazz, hip-hop, and maybe even some gymnastics. There are many more well-rounded dancers today who can do several styles well. This will give them a leg up at the audition, but remember, this is show *business* and most dancers have no clue about the *business* part of this industry.

Things like politics, marketing, etiquette, and money management never cross their mind. All they care about is getting a job dancing on a Lady Gaga music video. They are completely missing the chance to make a boat load of money.

Again, not to sound redundant, (or to keep shamelessly plugging our book) but this is why we wrote this book, created our seminars, and allowed ourselves to serve as a resource for the aspiring and already working dancer.

Now is the time to take advantage of this opportunity to get a leg up on the competition.

*N*ow is the time to *ACT!*

THE BUSINESS

EVERYTHING YOU NEED TO
KNOW ABOUT
THE HOLLYWOOD DANCE INDUSTRY OF DANCE

LEARN | BOOK | SUCCEED

CHAPTER ONE

Finding and Landing an Agent

*T*he most important person in a new dancer's career is their agent. Finding an agency who believes in you enough to consistently send you out on auditions is just the thing you need to fast track your career. One of the most common questions we get is, "Where can I find a dance agent?" Both of us could rattle off six or seven agencies, name the top agents, and provide the city, so that you could run off to do a Google search. But we usually answer the question with a question. "What are you looking to do?" "Do you want to be a hip-hop dancer in music videos?" "Do you want to go on commercial auditions?" "What exactly are you looking to get out of working as a dancer in the business?"

Most dancers don't think about these questions. They try to jump in and hope to figure it out as they go along. Big mistake! By not having a plan in the *beginning*, it wastes valuable time. Your window of opportunity as a dancer is short. By knowing what you want to do in the beginning, you will know which people to be around to maximize your career.

GETTING SIGNED

There are four main ways that agencies sign clients:

> *Referrals.* Any signed dancer or choreographer you meet could recommend you to his or her agency, and glowing recommendations from trusted clients is one way agencies sign new dancers.
> *Open auditions.* Major agencies hold two to four open auditions each year—advertised on agency websites and in major dance studios in L.A.

> *Cold submissions.* Dancers can submit themselves to the agency with a head shot, resume and sample of their work, such as a DVD of performance clips. However, know that

even with this sort of submission, you will usually be asked to come to a live audition as well. Keep in mind that your submission will be one of hundreds received in the mail each month, so include a cover letter with simple and straightforward bullet points outlining your training and major performance work.

> *Scouting.* Being in the right place at the right time has landed many professional dancers agency representation. Agents attend dance concert events, showcases, competitions and classes, looking for the next great dancer.

Now that you know how to get signed, let's talk about finding and booking a dance agent. The first step is to find them. We've done most of the work in finding a dance agent for you (You're welcome). Below is a list of the top dance agencies in Los Angeles (in no particular order).

Dorothy Day Otis (DDO)

Address: 6725 Sunset Blvd. Suite 230 Los Angeles, CA. 90028

Phone Number: (323) 462-8000

Website: www.ddoagency.com

> Represents: Choreographers, Dancers, Actors, and Models
> High Profile Clients include: Nancy O' Mera, Keri LeGrand, and Glen Douglas Packard
> Offices in: Los Angeles, New York, Las Vegas, and Nashville

---

BLOC Dance Agency

Address: 5651 Wilshire Blvd. Suite C. Los Angeles, CA. 90036

Phone Number: (323) 954-7730

Website: www.blocagency.com

- ➢ Represents: Choreographers, Dancers, Actors
- ➢ High profile clients: Fatima, Brian Friedman, and Rich & Tone
- ➢ Offices in: Los Angeles, Atlanta, and New York

McDonald, Selznick, and Associates (MSA)

Address: 953 Cole Ave. Los Angeles, CA. 90038

Phone Number: (323) 957-6680

Website: www.msaagency.com

- ➢ Represent: Choreographers, Dancers, Actors, Stage Directors, and Production Designers
- ➢ High Profile Clients: Kenny Ortega, Jamie King, Mia Michaels, and Wade Robson
- ➢ Offices: Los Angeles and New York

Clear Talent Group (CTG)

Address: 10950 Ventura Blvd. Studio City, CA. 91604

Phone Number: (818) 509-0121

Website: www.cleartalentgroup.com

- ➤ Represents the top Choreographers, Dancers, Actors, and Models in the business.
- ➤ High Profile Clients: Rosero and Jamal, Monie Adamson, and Tony Gonzalez.
- ➤ Offices in Los Angeles and New York.

TRIO Talent

Address: 1502 Gardner St. Los Angeles, CA. 90046

Phone Number: (323) 851-6886

Website: www.triotalentagency.com

- ➤ Represents: Choreographers and Dancers
- ➤ High Profile Clients: Frank Gatson, Dante Henderson, Ro Ro.
- ➤ Offices in: Los Angeles

Be sure to attend auditions for each dance agency on this list. As with anything, practice makes practiced. If you practice auditioning correctly, you will become better at this important skill. Some people will need all the practice that they can get. This means attend the audition, name drop (if you have a name to drop), make yourself stand out, and follow all the other steps we mention in the "Audition" section of our book. Keep in mind that it's nice to have several different agencies interested in representing you, but you will eventually sign with only one.

Let's get both the question and answer out of the way right now. We know you are asking yourself; "Which agency is better?" The truth is that they all are very good at what they do. What you are looking for is if the agent will work hard for you. You also need to consider these types of questions.

➢ Does the agent provide you personal attention, or are you simply a name on a paper?
➢ Are they quick to respond to your questions?
➢ Do you get a good feeling when you speak with them?
➢ Does the agent communicate with you after you land the job?
➢ Does this agent have access to people and opportunities that other agents do not?

These are some of the questions you need to consider. Go with your gut and remember that just as it is important for the agent to get to know you as a person, so to do you need to get to know them.

So there, you're done, right? All you have to do is call them up, ask them when their next audition is, go there, book it, and you're off to fame and riches, right? Wrong! Booking the agent is the easy part. You still have to do your marketing, research the choreographer, go to class to perfect your craft, etc. Keep in mind-the agency already has working dancers. Even if they bring you on, it's no guarantee that they will consistently send you out.

At this point, let's discuss what an agent CAN and CANNOT do for you:

An Agent CAN:

> **Get you into auditions.** The agent that you sign with will be able to assess your skills so that they can send you out on the jobs which you will give you a greater chance of success. When they receive a request for dancers, they will submit your photo to the production company. Your agent uses the agency name and relationship to try and get you opportunities. Though employers sometimes hold open auditions (cattle calls) to cast dancers for jobs; most are closed, meaning you need an agent to grant you access.

> **Negotiate your pay and contract.** Keeping track of the business details of your dance career can be simple if you have a full-year contract with a company. However, commercial dancers often juggle dozens of shorter jobs a month. Once you book a job, your agent will handle the financial and legal aspects, like negotiating pay, making sure you're paid on time and approving contracts. For tours, there are often 30- or 40-page contracts that dancers have to sign. Your agent is more than capable of looking over those contracts and trying to revise them if possible. They will make sure you're paid fairly, including overtime or double-time pay when needed and extra money when it's due—like if you're using your own wardrobe for a job, or working on a music video that will also be sold on the internet.

Keep in mind that most of the agent's work comes *after* you book the job. They *can* send you to auditions, they *cannot* help you with your networking, marketing, audition skills, or navigate you through the politics of the industry. This is why we say that agents get 10% of the pay. It's because they do 10% of the work, but the other 90% is left up to you. With this book and our seminars, we help you dramatically increase your odds.

How do you increase your chances of getting picked up by an agency?

1. Improve your chances by working on your look. As with any relationship, you only get one chance to make a first impression. Come to the audition looking like you are in the industry. Remember, it is a fashion show.

2. Bring a head shot. If you do not have one, get in touch with us, we have contacts with several photographers who can take a head shot for you quick and cheap. This is *not* the time to be spending lots of money on photos. Wait until *after* you land your agent.

3. Be sure you are ready to dance ballet, hip-hop, and Jazz at the audition. This means you may have to brush up on your technique. If you are strictly a street dancer, be sure you do not appear at the jazz audition by mistake.

4. Learn the art of the name drop. One of the easiest ways to do this is by dropping a name. Name dropping in a subtle and not-so-obvious way is an important skill to master. The industry is driven by relationships, so *who* you know is just as important as *how* well you dance. Take a class from an agency-represented choreographer. Before you leave, find out what agency they are represented by. When you audition for that agency, you can then say to the agent, "Thank you very much for the opportunity, I just took class with so and so and they said this was a great agency to be represented by, that's why I'm here." Not only do you give love to the agency and agent, but you also build rapport by discussing a common person: the choreographer that you took class from. You have made an impression on the agent and now you are up on the competition!

DON'T BE A STRANGER!

Many dancers think that once they find representation, they can just sit back and wait for the auditions to start pouring in. Nothing could be further from the truth. Signing with an agent is a major step forward that signals a new phase in your career, but it doesn't mean you get to stop being an active participant. If anything, this is the time to increase your efforts.

Here's what you need to understand: When you first sign with a dance agency, you're nothing more than a name on a list. Unless you bring a lot of credits and contacts to the table, your agents will view you as the new dancer in a certain age category, and that's about it. Naturally, they have every intention of working for you, but like it or not, you're the new client whom no one really knows. In a sense, you're being given a blank slate to prove yourself, both as a dancer and as a person. And this is where most of you drop the ball by disappearing off the face of the planet.

We can't begin to tell you how many times we've met talented dancers that do nothing more than land an agent. An agent friend of ours once told us that she auditioned a dancer who made a terrific impression. Excited, she introduced him to the other agents in the office, who liked him, too. They agreed to represent the guy, hoping their instincts pay off. The dancer came in with an excited smile pasted on his face, signed the contract, dropped off his pictures and resumes, and then he was gone—never to be heard from again.

If you want to have a successful relationship with your new agents, you have to give them a chance to get to know you as a person, not just as a dancer. That's how you become more than a name on a list. If your agents start seeing you as a real human being, with a life outside the industry, they'll be more likely to start working harder for you. "Needy dancers with no lives are boring to us," Our agent friend told us, "Real people aren't."

Now don't get us wrong. We're not suggesting you act like a pest, dropping by the office all the time, calling every hour to ask what's going on. That would be a major mistake. You need to be smart about how you cultivate a relationship with your new reps.

Here's our advice: Invite each of your agents to lunch, one at a time, so you get some valuable face time with everyone. Just don't waste this golden opportunity by talking about your career. Instead, try to create an environment where there's a lot of back-and-forth about each other. Ask as many questions as you answer. Get to know each other as people. You want your agent to go back to the office and tell everyone how much fun he or she had at lunch with you. Trust us, that kind of positive energy will pay off big time.

You can also find excuses to drop by the office every now and then, so you can see your agents in person. For example, you can stop by reception to tell your agent how your audition for the Academy Awards went. Of course your agent will step out of their office to say hello and hear the great feedback. By doing that, you show your agent your gratitude for the opportunity, and that makes them feel good as a person. Mission accomplished.

Remember, agents get 10 percent as commission from any work you do, while you get 90 percent. So, you have to work harder than them if you're going to succeed, which means staying in class, having great head shots, networking, doing well at auditions, and, most of all, being more than a name on your agent's list.

As we stated earlier in this chapter, getting an agent is not that difficult. Heck, we've even provided you the names and addresses of the top dance agencies in Los Angeles. An agent can help you get into an audition as well as negotiate your pay and contract. They cannot help you with networking, politics, and your audition skills- that is entirely up to you. Once you get your agent, you will need to take some new head shots. What does a good photographer charge? Where can you find one? How do you create a resume when you have no credits? These and many more questions will be answered in the next chapter.

CHAPTER TWO

Headshots & Resumes

Your head shot speaks for you after the audition is over. When the room is empty, your head shot is laid on the floor or table among other dancers who made the final cut. Hiring decisions are made based on the things not in your control. Height, color, tattoos, ethnicity, sex all come into play. How sad would it be for you if the choreographer found your name in the pile but instead of your photo, there is a piece of scratch paper with your name, height, and ethnicity on it?

Many times in this book, we will stress to you the importance of building good relationships with everyone you come in contact with in the entertainment business. *Always* look at the people you meet as your potential boss. This is true of your photographer as well. Let's be frank, you're going to need good head shots. You're going to need other photos as well: 3/4, full body, fashion, and action. Having a good photographer that you trust on your team will go a long way towards building that image you want.

We suggest taking new photos often, once every three – six months, if you can. Taking photos often gets you comfortable working in front of the camera, which will benefit you if you decide to act or model. Next, when you meet with your agent, and show them your new shots, it gets them excited about sending you out again. Lastly, it provides you flexibility when you are being submitted for work. Nothing kills opportunity more then head shots with the same smiling head wearing different clothing.

In the beginning, we suggest you use one of the photographers provided to you by the agency. They are approved and trusted by your agent. Using their photographer will ensure your agency likes your pictures- and then you won't have to do them over if they don't like them. Don't spend more than $350 for head shots. For that price, you should be getting no less than 2 rolls, or 48 photos (A roll contains 24 shots).

Some photographers are good at telling you what to wear, but many are not. Our suggestion is have an idea of what you want to portray in your photos and stick to your plan. Remember that these shots are going to be what casting agents, directors, and others are going to see and will help you book work. Bring different types of clothing and be prepared to change a few looks with your hair. Don't be afraid to show off your assets, which may be chest or stomach for adult guys, or breasts and/or legs for adult women. For kids, it's about looking cute. The casting agent needs to believe that you can sell that toothpaste, Pop Tart, or KidzBop music CD.

Prepare to take an action shot. This is a shot with you in motion. This could be jumping, kicking, or some other acrobatic maneuver. (You may not use the action shot in your final headshot, but it's good to have just in case). Also prepare a beauty shot. This is a shot showing you looking cool, sexy, and stylish. If you don't have one, practice on your sexy looks. It would be a good idea to have a couple of outfits pre-chosen for this shot so that you don't waste time. You should also prepare a commercial shot. That is a clean-cut look with you smiling. This can be used for mainstream and commercial products. *Note*: Practice on your smile and sexy look prior to the shoot. Use that handy camera phone to "test" what you will look like.

If you are not a fashionista , bring along a friend who is. They can help keep your look fun and will shorten the photo shoot time. Prepare to spend a good four hours of your day shooting. Many photographers will have someone at the shoot to do your hair and makeup (the $350 should include this service). If you are confident in doing your own hair and makeup, tell your photographer in the beginning. You may be able to lower the cost of your session, because the photographer will not need to hire someone. If you know in advance when you will be shooting, make it a point to watch your diet, hit the gym, and get plenty of rest the night before your shoot. These shots are important, so you want to be at your best!

Once you take the photos, you will pick up sheets or a CD from your photographer. These sheets have 24 small, thumbnail-sized photos on each page. A good photographer will mark the shots they believe work for you. However, this does not mean that you have to use them as your final headshot. Once you pick the sheets up, examine them and have five or six in mind that you would like to highlight to your agent. Schedule a sit down meeting with your agent so that they can view the photos for themselves. They will pick five or six shots that they will want to have you uploaded to L.A. Casting. This website is utilized by many production companies because they can get the specific look and type casted without having to hold a bunch of 8x10 photos. You will also need to create a hard copy of your shots, usually in the form of a zed card. A zed card is smaller than an 8x10 (5x7). They possess a large head shot on the front and three - four different "looks" on the back. This is important and a very valuable tool. Keep in mind; you'll be taking photos often, with a variety of different looks. You can change your zed card as you continue to take photos (rather cheaply). We would advise you to consider changing the card every eight – nine months. Also, you can upload your new looks onto L.A. Casting.

ZED CARD

Chali Jennings
Height: 5'9" Bust: 34c Waist: 26 Hips: 36 Hair: Dark Blonde Eyes: Brown Shoe: 9 Dress 4-6

Once the photos are chosen, you may need to take them to a re-finisher. A re-toucher can remove imperfections and blemishes or to make your eyes pop. There is an extra charge for this service (between $70 - $100), but it's well worth it. Murphy's Law says that anything that can go wrong will, and the day of your photo shoot is no exception. Expect to have that pimple on the tip of your nose appear on photo shoot day. A re-toucher is so beneficial, because they can remove that and any other imperfections!

before   after

Photo Retouching by RA Retouching

Since you will take photos once every three – four months, it is good to develop a relationship with a good photographer. Initially, you would ideally want to use a photographer your agent trusts, but as you begin to build your portfolio of looks, it would be wise to branch out and establish relationships with other photographers. Many new photographers are trying to build a portfolio, which is perfect for you! In many of those cases, their fees will be reduced, and, in some cases, free! But you need to be careful and only use a photographer you know and trust. This is the entertainment business and some individuals are looking to prey on unsuspecting aspiring artists. Whenever possible, take a friend with you for both support and protection.

RESUMES

When getting started, you will still need a resume to go along with your picture to show the choreographer or director that you have experience. We can hear you wondering, "How do I put together a resume without having professional experience?" You just have to be creative by taking what you have and making it sound more exciting. If you performed in your local dance studio recital, don't put: "Hip Hop number at Johns Dance Studio."

Name the event or production and then use the name of the theater or venue to make it sound more prestigious. If the studio recital was called, "Dancing under the Big Top" list on your resume as:

Under the Big Top   Dancer   Robert B. Moore Theater

There are usually three to four sections in a dance resume: Stage, Television/Film, Commercial, and Training. Once you get a few jobs under your belt, you can separate Television from Film and add more categories, for example, Music Videos.

List all special skills like Sports, Tumbling, Break Dancing, Skating, etc., and always put your training on the bottom of the resume.

Make sure that you update your resume as soon as you finish a job, so that the next time you audition you have more current bookings on your resume. List production studios, networks, and choreographers you have worked with. This is especially important in the beginning of your career, because if a decision maker doesn't know you, they may discern your talent based on who has hired you in the past.

On the next page is an example of a resume format that MSA approved for Tim: (Notice next to commercials, it states: "List available upon request." This is a good tool to use when you have not had commercial jobs. It sounds like you have too many to list.) Also, he has too many credits to list on one page, see we had to scale it back.

1611A NORTH EL CENTRO   HOLLYWOOD, CA 90028

TEL: 323-957-6680 FAX: 323-957-5694

Tim Stevenson

HEIGHT: 5'10

EYES: Brown

HAIR COLOR: Black

FILM

| Bringing Down The House | Dancer | Adam Shankman |

TELEVISION

| MTV Awards – Jennifer Lopez | Dancer | MTV Networks |

COMMERCIALS

List available upon request.

STAGE/LIVE PERFORMANCE

| Today Show – Jennifer Lopez | Dancer | CBS Prod |

TRAINING

Acting: Elaine Hall-Katz, Edward Baker, Nancy Mott

SPECIAL SKILLS

Singing, Soccer, Football, Snowboarding, Baseball, Wake Boarding

As we discussed, your head shots should cost no more than $350 (less, if possible). Your first session should be with a photographer your agent trusts. Once you and your agent chose the photos, upload them to L.A. Casting (www.lacasting.com) and create your zed card. With your newly completed resume in hand, you are now ready to attend your first audition! What should you expect? How should you dress? How do you get noticed? The next chapter is one of the most important in this book. We suggest you read it twice!

*R*innnng! The phone call just came in from your agent. The audition is tomorrow at Debbie Reynolds for a Nike commercial. The choreographer is Hi-Hat and it pays enough to make your rent next month.

Your heart leaps! Sweet! You can hardly wait to kill it tomorrow.

The day of the audition, you wake up early because of your excitement. You're planning on getting there early, getting a good parking spot and taking some time to scope out the competition. You hit the gym early, pick the perfect outfit, and put the finishing touches on your hair and makeup (What? You've never seen a guy with makeup on at an audition?).

At the audition, you learn the choreography, practice on the side, and do your thing. You make it past the first cut. Now the decision makers show up. You do the steps; add a little freestyle in the beginning and at the end of the routine to draw attention to yourself....BAM!! You are now in the last group....You're getting closer!

After a couple more times, the choreographer's assistant puts everyone in a straight line. All the players sit at the table and look at head shots in front of you. You wait as you watch the assistant speak to the group at the table, walk over to the dancer at the end, and whisper something in their ear, causing the dancer to either stay or leave. This happens one after the other, until finally they get to you. You're hoping not to hear the dreaded, "Thank you very much" whispered into your ear.

After final looks, everyone is let go and the choreographer explains that if they are interested, they will contact your agent.

You haven't booked the job yet, but you definitely rocked the audition.

How do you increase your possibility of being THE one that gets that call? In this chapter, we will discuss several things that can increase your odds.

This chapter is so important; we want you to read it twice BEFORE going to the next chapter. Read it twice because there's a lot of information we're going to cover. Read it twice because you as a new dancer are just another face in the crowd, and this chapter will help you leap over the hundreds of dancers that do not apply these guidelines. Read it twice because your career depends on it. After all, auditions are the first time a director, producer, or choreographer will see you live. It's their first impression of you. In fact, it's so important that Tim and I will start from the very beginning- receiving the call from your agent.

What's the first thing you should do once you get the call from your agent?

DO YOUR RESEARCH ON THE CHOREOGRAPHER OR PRODUCT.

A good dancer knows what to expect. Doing your research beforehand, so you know the style, temperament, and personality of the choreographer will give you a better understanding of what to expect at the audition and what to say to the choreographer. An advertiser, choreographer, or director needs to feel comfortable that you will help convey the overall message and make the product more marketable. In this day of YouTube and Google, there is no reason why any dancer should not be able to do research on a product or person. Researching a product online will help you with everything from your dress style to the type of personality you should bring to the audition. Be prepared!

ACTING IS KEY!

For all auditions, but especially for commercials, you need to bring your "A" personality. We highly suggest taking at least one commercial acting class every other week. Just as you need to strengthen your physical body, you need to enhance your "Acting Muscle" as well. Having a personality that draws people to you or makes it a pleasure to have you on the set is one of the benefits to taking acting classes. Additionally, dancing *is* acting with movement. So, not only are you helping your dance performance level, but you are also making yourself more marketable by being a double threat. Now, if you could only sing...

YOUR LOOK IS FIRST, YOUR SKILLS ARE SECOND.

You might be surprised to learn that the most important criteria for booking the job in Hollywood is not how high you can kick or how many pirouettes you can whip out. As a Hollywood dancer, your *look* is the most important factor in booking a job. So what you wear and how you style yourself needs to be a priority before you go on the audition.

Your agent tells you to "Dress body conscious" or "Dress ready to dance." What the heck does that mean? It means to think about your clothing for the audition, and to dress according to your audience. When you consider who or what you auditioning for, these phrases can take on a different meaning. Whatever you wear, it needs to show off your physical assets and give you the freedom to move. This is particularly true if you are dancing for a younger choreographer, because they are usually following today's latest trends and they are focused on what's hot right now. Most of the time, they are looking for people who fit the specific look they have in mind for the job. If you're dancing for an older choreographer, then your look is not as important, because older choreographers tend to care more about what you can deliver as opposed to how cute your outfit is. Although you still need to look your best, you could get away with dressing in a more classical, "New York" style (tights, leotards, etc). Based on our personal experiences, we would still suggest dressing up, as the choreographer does not always have the final say on who will or will not book the job. The director, producer, actor, or singer may also have a say in this decision. We talk about how these individuals will have a direct impact on your career later in this book, but keep in mind; these are major players that also need to be impressed. Instead of talent, this group tends to focus on people who catch their eye or are attractive. They know nothing about dance, so look is important.

Courtney will never forget the time he was auditioning for Janet Jackson. It was a huge audition outside of Los Angeles which put him up was up against 400 or so other male dancers. Every guy was dressed (or undressed) in tight shirts or topless, because they knew their *look* was important. After about two hours of auditioning, he made it to the final group. At the very end, Janet came in (with her dark glasses) and sat behind the table with the choreographer and several dancers who had already booked the job. They asked the final 30 guys to get in one line. As Janet and her choreographer were reviewing head shots, the person that he was standing next to leaned forward, turned to his friend and, talking about one of the outfits of a guy auditioning, whispered with a slight lisp, and stated:

"I have two words for you: ***crushed velvet***."

Folks, that's all she wrote! This guy had nothing on but the shoes on his feet and a pair of maroon, crushed velvet hot pants. The outfit did what it was supposed to do. It brought him attention. On top of that, he was a good dancer. See the benefit of being mindful of your look? He did not book the job, but his whole package (and I am using that term loosely) helped increase his odds.

You will not book 100% of the auditions you attend. There are too many variables. Are you the right height? The right color? What are your dance skills? What is your look? Your personality? Ultimately, what you are trying to do is increase your odds so that you can be in that final discussion at the end of the audition. A choreographer friend of mine has a certain thought process when it comes to choosing dancers for his projects. For the most part, his artists (Beyonce, Tyrese, En Vogue and others) are squeaky clean, all-American performers. He hires good looking, clean-cut dancers. He understands that the dancers are a reflection of the artist. After auditions for Destiny's Child, we would lay the headshots on the floor to pick dancers. Comments would be made on each photo: "What about this one?" "No, he looks too gay." or "No, he has too many tattoos and piercings." or "He needs to do something with his hair." Since the dancer is the reflection of the artist, you need to know what the choreographer is looking for prior to the audition and transform your look accordingly. This is why the research is so important! Sometimes, you have to be a chameleon, a Madonna when it comes to auditions. Dancers that can go from edgy to clean-cut will work the most. Keep in mind that the grungy, edgy look is only good for a few artists and brands. You would truly be limiting yourself if that was your only look. Your head shot and zed card should reflect different looks. Another good idea is to bring a second set of clothing just in case you need to change your look. Ladies, we would highly suggest bringing some heels to the audition because you never know if you may need them!

Now, you are ready for the audition. You've done research and you have your look down. When should you audition? Some people like to audition in the first group, others, in the last group. Does it matter? Read on and find out!

TIMING

Timing is probably more important than you think. Auditioning early in the day could help you because the casting agent or choreographer is fresh. On the other hand, shining in the last group of the day, after the choreographer has seen a bunch of "duds," could be the ticket to landing the job. This isn't an exact science, so along with our tips and personal experiences, you'll have to use your judgment to make the best decision.

Auditioning at the beginning can be a great advantage for you because the choreographers/directors and or casting people are awake and ready to be impressed. They're not tired from watching dancers all day, thus overly critical and ready to cut dancers too quickly in an effort to go home early. Knowing who is casting can also be an important factor in what time to audition. Some choreographers may like to pick from those first groups, while others may be energized after seeing lots of different dancers. Again, do your homework to know what is right for each job. You will learn which time is better through trial and error, knowing the choreographer and casting directors, and knowing yourself.

Once, when Tim was auditioning for a major artist, he decided to arrive over an hour early to avoid the barrage of dancers hoping to be the first person that the production company saw for the job. When he arrived, he wasn't the first person in line, but he was in the first group of twenty people to sign in on the sheet. As the audition hour grew close, hundreds of other dancers started showing up. He said, "Wow! Lots of peeps for one spot!" The audition began and he was one of 40 other dancers in the first group in the room. Even though he knew there were other great dancers in the room, he was very confident about his ability. He drew the attention of the decision makers and impressed them early. Since there were only thirty-nine other dancers to compare him to, the choreographers had not been jaded by all the bad dancers or six hours worth of auditions. He made it past the first two cuts with ease and landed the callback scheduled for later that day.

Consider this: He got in early, impressed the choreographers, and was able to watch as talented dancers perform and entire groups of 10 were cut. Since this was an audition for a major artist, the huge cattle call meant a long day for choreographers, getting fatigued by looking at all the dancers. Every dancer starts to look the same, and the choreographer just wants to wrap everything up and get out of there.

His early start meant that he was in the top 8 out of the original 200+ men. Not too shabby. In the second round, the artist was in the viewing room behind a shade, choosing the dancers herself. He got kept again- now he's in the top five! We do the routine again and again and again. BAM! Top 3! All the dancers left are amazing. Who do they choose now?

At this point in the audition process, the dancer has done their job. The ultimate goal is to book the gig, but in order to do this; you need to be in the final conversation. But, auditioning first allowed Tim to get past the competition and land in the top three.

A word of caution: When you audition early, be careful to pace yourself. We have seen many dancers not only performing during their audition, but also practicing full out on the sides. After a long day, they begin to forget the steps while in the final groups! That's the *worst* time to blank out. Near the end, you are auditioning with a small group of amazing dancers. The artist, the choreographer, and sometimes the director, are watching you. This is not the time to be forgetting steps! You *will* lose the job. So, don't dance full out when you are not auditioning unless you are still in the room. Word of wisdom: The audition really begins the minute you step into the room. When you are on the sides, rotate between marking the steps and watching the other dancers. You will learn much from just watching. In fact, watching the dancers and the reaction of the choreographer may help you, because you may be able to take what is working and discard what isn't.

That's a lot of information to digest, so let's take a time out and summarize.

To summarize:

> ➢ Pros to auditioning early: You are compared against fewer dancers, increasing your chances of making it to next round. Judges are fresh and not in a hurry to leave. You have time to study what works and doesn't work by watching judges' reactions.
> ➢ Cons to auditioning early: You increase your chances of fatigue. You are more likely to begin forgetting the steps.

Our advice: Best to audition early at *large auditions*.

However, sometimes auditioning at the end can work to your benefit. From our experience, it can be to your advantage to audition in the last group if the audition is small. The decision makers are relatively "fresh". At times we have been chosen because we were a refreshing change at the end of the audition. The choreographer may have been seeing the same style of dancer all day, and you can come along and wake them up from the judging coma they've been in for the past couple of hours. As we referenced before, you will learn more by trial and error. Each situation is different, and there is no perfect remedy.

Something that you will not have at smaller auditions is the opportunity to review the steps many times over. You don't have the huge number of dancers auditioning in small groups that you can watch over and over again. Most of the time, you just learn the steps and perform. If it normally takes time for you to pick up choreography, that could be a problem. Another problem with smaller auditions is that you may not have an opportunity to read the reaction of the choreographer or casting agent. In many cases, non-verbal communication (facial expressions, posture, crossing of the arms, the reaction of the eyes) tells you a lot about how a person feels about something. You may not be able to utilize these tools at a small audition.

If an audition if really small, it will just be you, a casting agent, and a camera. They will have you freestyle to 30 seconds of music. If they allow you to go longer than 30 seconds, that may mean they like what they see! Keep in mind, the person recording you may not have a say in your hiring. In most cases, there is a choreographer or director who will review the tape and make the decision.

To review (If audition is small):

➤ Pros to auditioning late: No judge fatigue. You may be a great change of pace from what they've seen throughout the day.

➤ Cons to auditioning late: You may have to pick up the choreography faster. You may have to freestyle. If you are put on camera, you will not be able to read the reaction of the decision maker.

Personally, we like to audition at the beginning because it puts the focus and attention on us early in the day. This allows us to set the bar high so that if others can't reach it, the job is ours. Like Tiger Woods on a Sunday with his famous red shirt, we go for blood early!

FLOOR ETIQUETTE

Every audition has a standard floor etiquette every dancer is expected to follow. Meaning, you are courteous to your fellow dancer. You switch lines when asked by the choreographer. You are aware of other dancer's personal space. Is this usually followed during an audition?

Ha! Most dancers forget everything mentioned once they walk into the room. It is dog-eat-dog and you better be in the correct mind-set. You will fall victim to such negative things as: Dancers standing directly in front of you to get one up on the competition. The dancer who dances full out in a crowded room while learning, and bumps you repeatedly without saying sorry. The dancer who pushes you aside thinking you are beneath them, etc. A good choreographer will rotate lines in the room, but it doesn't mean people will move.

You need to be assertive (but not overly aggressive) in a professional manner, or you will get lost in the mix. For example, when rotating lines from the front, don't go to the far back if you still do not understand the steps, go to the middle. When there are hundreds of people at your audition, it may be necessary to move your way to the front of the room so you can see how the choreographer is doing the steps. Your best bet is to arrive early (especially for large auditions), so you can be one of the first in the room and not have to fight as much.

We do believe that good floor etiquette is important for each dancer to display toward each other. It's a sign of respect. If you do come across a rude dancer, there are some things to remember:

If you are bumped by another dancer, its okay to kindly let them know about it. Sometimes, they honestly don't realize they have bumped into someone because they are so focused in on trying to pick up the choreography. Most people will immediately apologize. However, you may come across a person who is rude enough to say, "Get out of my way!" In that case, it's okay to stand your ground and let them know that they came into your space. Don't spend too much time going back and forth; you still have choreography to learn. Let your dancing do the "talking" for you!

If you are truly lost, don't be afraid to ask a question. Be sure to listen if another dancer asks a question so that you do not repeat the same question. We know that this is exactly what your teacher from your local studio has been preaching for the past 13 years of your life, but it is the truth. Listen to the questions other dancers pose. You will run the risk of being overlooked if you repeat questions because the choreographer will think that your behavior in an audition will transfer to the set. They simply do not have time to waste answering the same question over and over again. As a result, you will lose that job.

Auditioning in a room that is crammed with dancers can be difficult. If you do not have enough space to dance full out, don't dance full out. Respect other dancers space; understanding that they are just as crammed as you. This means, you may not be able to fully extend your arm, kick, or jump. Save that for your smaller groups. Once the choreographer places you in a smaller group, use that time to dance full out, and work out the kinks. If you are not clear on the steps, be sure to ask before it really counts.

GETTING NOTICED

This section may seem like a no-brainer. Of course, the best way to get noticed is by being an incredible dancer, right?

Although your technique matters, the best dancers are not the ones who always book the job. We will say that again: THE BEST DANCERS ARE NOT THE ONES WHO ALWAYS BOOK THE JOB.

There, now that we've got that off our chests, let us explain why that is, and what a person needs to do at the audition to get noticed.

Have you ever danced in class with someone who has amazing technique? They can routinely hit six, seven, or eight pirouettes. They are amazingly limber. They have all the technical skills in the world. But they never book jobs. Or if they do, it's once in a while, and only certain types?

There is a simple explanation to this. To find out why, take this simple test and see if you know the answers. Check your answers below:

> How many pirouettes do you typically perform at an audition?
> What side do you typically have to kick on?
> What's the hardest technical sequence you typically have to do at an audition?

If you check your answers below, you will be very surprised to know how little skill you actually have to display at an audition.

Answers: Two pirouettes, right side, double pirouette jump out (stick it with both feet)

As you can see, very little technique is needed at many auditions. This doesn't mean that you don't try to perfect your craft. In fact, we suggest you learn several styles well. In order to get noticed, a dancer needs to be strong at *multiple* styles. Just as a body builder works on different sets of muscles to strengthen the whole body, a dancer should learn different styles to strengthen their marketability. This will assure you are not stuck being known only as a jazz, hip-hop, or specialty dancer. Too many times, dancers shoot themselves in the foot because they are so limited in their dancing.

Being able to take on any style of dance at any audition is a tremendous asset to your career .If you can bust out the jazz, the ballet, the lyrical and the hip hop at any given time, then you are golden and will be sent out on more calls. Versatility is key!

A common mistake of limited dancers is that they perform the wrong style at the wrong time. Courtney once held a hip-hop audition for a Disney television show. He had the dancers dance twice, switching lines each time. After they danced the second time, He had them freestyle. Let us repeat this again: this was a hip-hop audition. When a dancer is asked to free-style, they typically perform their strongest style. We can't tell you how many dancers free-styled *jazz* at my *hip-hop* audition. Guess who didn't make it past the first cut?

Confidence, eye contact, and "fire" (meaning energy), high-level execution of the steps, and personality are *huge* at getting you noticed. "Fire" and energy can put you above the rest. Anyone can do the steps, but not everyone can put their special fire and energy in the steps. Your confidence will be a lot more genuine if you know several different styles. This means being able to freestyle in each of these styles. Eye contact with the people who make the decisions helps to portray confidence. Don't be afraid to work the room. Have fun with each of the decision makers while you dance. This doesn't mean changing the choreographer's choreography (they hate that, by the way) but it does mean adding an extra hair whip, facial expression, or other movement that keeps the integrity of the steps, but adds an extra twist. If you do not know how to do this, the next time you take class; try to add something different without changing the fundamental steps. Be sure to practice this in every class until it is second nature.

Have you ever heard of a person who was afraid of heights who decided to conquer that fear by sky diving, or bungee jumping off a bridge? No doubt they were screaming on the way down, but the experience slowly helped them get over their fear. Something similar happens when some new dancers go to auditions early in their career. They notice that some of the dancers they are auditioning against are the same people they have been idolizing. Star struck, their performance suffers due to fear and lack of confidence. You should look forward to stretching yourself by dancing next to talented dancers. We know most people don't want to stand next to an amazing dancer. Being afraid to dance next a talented dancer is a legitimate concern. But that may be just the thing you need to help push you to the next level. We are big Laker fans. From time to time, the Lakers lose to teams they should beat easily. Why? Because the prospect of having to play one of the best teams in the league makes the not-so-talented teams try harder. This could be due to pride, desire, or maybe the bad team was not playing to their ability up to that point. Whatever the reason, they give the Lakers their best whenever they play them.

When we were dancing, we called that "pulling up," a term typically used when you pirouette. "Pulling up" meant that the individual had or needed to improve their performance. This theory can ring true for you as well during the audition process. We would always stand next to the best because it made us "pull up" our performance at an audition. This helped us become better dancers more quickly, and, eventually, two of the best in the business. We would stand next to dancers that we knew could out dance us, but over time as we improved, we became the ones who people didn't want to stand next to. Just like anything else, you emulate the best to become the best. Have the confidence to dance next to whoever is in the room and go for it. Your confidence will greatly improve. It's survival of the fittest in this business so have the drive to be there.

Today, many dancers can perform several styles of dance. What was unique 10 years ago is becoming more commonplace. This is why you need to always be in class perfecting your craft. Many dancers are good at jazz, hip-hop, and ballet. Gymnastics will help you stand out. Courtney first started dancing during the time of Madonna, Michael, Janet, and Paula. It was a time when jazz was really big. He was a hip-hop dancer when he first started. His agent even called him a hip-hop dancer. He knew that he always wanted to dance with MJ and thought the only way that that was going to happen was if he learned jazz. For 3 years, he focused only on ballet (the basis for all dance forms) and modern. He eventually got his stretch past the splits. His strength and confidence went through the roof. By the time he finished high school, he was able to go to any audition, from jazz, to ballet, to hip-hop, and excelled at all three. Even when he did not book the job, he stood out because people began to understand that he was a threat in any style of dance. He only wishes he had learned gymnastics, because that would have truly made him complete.

The bottom line:

- ➢ Your look is just as important as your dancing.
- ➢ Research the person or product you are auditioning for.
- ➢ Be sure to work the people auditioning you.
- ➢ Thank the choreographer and other decision makers on your way out.

By mastering these things, you will increase your odds when you audition.

FREESTYLE

Here is a little known secret. Freestyle is 40 – 50 percent of what is necessary to book a job. Your ability to freestyle in multiple forms of dance is an important tool in the business. Most, but not all, auditions will ask you to freestyle at some point to see what you can create off the top of your head. We have even been to auditions where they don't teach you any steps; they only ask you to freestyle. If you can't, you're making it harder for yourself. It's also helpful because at the end of auditions, even when they teach you steps, you are typically asked to freestyle. I've seen dancers who were horrible doing the actual steps, book the job based on freestyle alone. You should practice this as much as you practice your technique in class. In essence, it's another style or technique.

We know many dancers don't think it's important or they feel awkward when free styling. Keep in mind that freestyle could be the defining factor in whether or not you get a job. If you feel your freestyle is a weak point in your dance vocabulary, then, like anything else, practice your craft. There will be auditions where the freestyle will come first and will determine if you get kept for the next round. You will get cut in the first round without strong freestyle! Take what you know well like turns, leaps, kicks, popping, break dancing, or krumpin' and practice doing what feels good off the top of your head. The more you practice at home or during dance classes, the easier it will become. In addition to this, one other tool you can use is gymnastics. We've been to auditions where the dancer forgot the steps, did a flip sequence, and booked the job. It's good to combine different styles when you freestyle. Hip-hop, jazz, and gymnastics, all done well, makes it hard to deny you the job.

TYPE CASTING

Typecasting is necessary to allow a choreographer, producer, or casting agent an easy way to decipher whom they want to see at an audition. The client calls the agency and the agency submits pictures. The client does a typecast so they don't get the people they don't need at the audition. They may only want blondes between 5'4 and 5'6 or African-American men who look between the ages of 16 – 19. The best way to use typecasting is to review and make decisions prior to calling the dancers in for the audition. With L.A. Casting, this has made the process much easier. From time to time, some jobs may not typecast until you show up at the audition. It's one of our biggest pet peeves. Tim lived in Orange County and there's nothing worse than driving the hour-plus drive to Hollywood after calling in sick to his job, getting a sub for his dance class, getting his mind and body prepped for the audition, standing in line, and before even learning a step, the choreographers say, "Thank you for coming." It was a waste of time- they could have cut him through picture submissions. Bottom line, as we will say repeatedly in this book. You're ability to book a job is part looks, part personality, part relationships, and part dance ability. It's *not* only about your dancing.

AFTER THE AUDITION

After the audition, do not leave immediately like other dancers. Go up to the choreographer or casting agent, thank them for their time by name, shake hands, smile, make eye contact and leave the room. You want to burn your face in their mind, so that after a long day of work, they will remember the one person who shook hands, smiled, and said their name. Remember, you are *always* planting the seed for the next time you see this person who is on the other side of the desk at an audition. Do your part in helping them remember you. Go to every audition. Smile. Perform. Thank them. Leave.

Here is some insight as to what happens after the audition is over and everyone has gone home. If the choreographer has not already pre-selected every spot with his or her friends, all of the photos are laid on the table or floor. At this point, all the dancers are good, so it's their look, height, ethnicity, and other things that are out of their control that will determine if they book this job. They will group similar looks together; blondes with blondes, Asians with Asians, boys with boys, etc. Then, they consider:

- ➢ Who is the artist? (Probably do not want another hot blonde dancing next to Britney Spears)
- ➢ How tall is the dancer? (Christina Aguilera is very short. She can't have tall women dancing around her, can she?)
- ➢ Is the artist or product edgy or clean cut? (Unless it's necessary, excessive tattoos, piercings, and hair cuts will limit your work. Save those looks for your headshot or zed card.)
- ➢ What is the dancer's reputation? (Dancers that are known to be hard to work with will have fewer opportunities no matter how good they are.)

There are many other things that are discussed or thought of which have nothing to do with dance. This is where body type and politics creep in. Other areas that may be considered: how sexy is the dancer, what are the chances of sleeping with them, etc. These are not considered by every choreographer, casting agent, or director, but understand, these thoughts are real. It isn't fair, but as we have been reminding you, the Hollywood dance scene is about more than just your talent.

We've covered a lot of information so far. See why we asked you to read this chapter twice? Below are some rules to follow at an audition:

RULES TO REMEMBER

1. Be in the front.

2. Be confident as soon as you walk in the door.

3. Come prepared for changes.

4. Bring clothing options.

5. Bring several types of shoes (mainly ladies).

6. More than one headshot and resume (You never know who else you will run into.).

7. Be on time- even if the choreographer isn't.

8. Say hello or be vocal, if possible. Remember, you're trying to leave an impression.

9. Be careful about what you say out loud at an audition (You never know who's listening.).

10. Try not to mark the dance steps unless it's crowded (or you are on the side of the room).

11. Be respectful to other dancers, because you never know if that dancer is a choreographer or a friend of the choreographer/director who's holding the audition.

12. Pace yourself. Don't suffer from fatigue and start to forget the steps at the end. That is the most important time of the audition.

13. Have fun. Practice on the side. Push for perfection.

14. If you mess up, don't you dare stop dancing! Pull focus and do something BIG (This is where freestyle can save you.). Just don't make the same mistake twice.

15. When you do a dance and it's time to be sexy, be sexy (If you don't know how, we suggest you practice at home in front of a mirror. This goes for both men and women.).

16. Be sure to pull focus when in your small group by dancing before and after you dance the routine.

GO TO ALL AUDITIONS

According to the book "Outliers", it takes 10,000 hours to master anything. If a dancer dances four hours a day every day, that would be almost seven years before they've mastered that style. The point we're trying to make is that you should make it a habit of attending as many auditions as possible. In fact, attend every audition. Never crash auditions (choreographers hate that and they do have long memories!).

Do not get in the habit of missing auditions. You would be cheating yourself out of experience, networking opportunities, and a possible job. In addition, if your agent finds out too many times, they will stop sending you out.

When you do attend an audition, be of this mindset: You are there to get this job. They may have already promised the gig to a friend. They may only have 4 dancers in mind. Your job is to make them *change their mind.*

We have gone to auditions where our agents mistakenly sent us, only to book the job. That's our job as dancers - to change minds. At one audition in particular that Courtney attended, they were looking for Hispanic men who could perform salsa dancing with a partner. He didn't care if he needed to dance Folklorico around a sombrero, he was after one thing, and that's a job! Courtney is neither Hispanic, nor had he ever danced salsa at the time. And to boot, he was barely 18, and this was more of an adult job. But he changed the mind of the choreographer, and to this date, he will forever be grateful to Dori Sanchez and Bubba Carr for giving a hip-hop dancing, black kid from Gardena an opportunity to dance on the Desi Awards with Tito Puente and many other Latin music stars.

Once again, it is your responsibility to *change their mind* at the audition. This is your job as a dancer.

Under 18 Note:

If you are either 16 or 17, and a very good dancer, ask your agent to send you out on the adult auditions. Why? Remember the 10,000 hour rule? You need the experience. Also, it helps you build a relationship with the choreographer. If you dance next to better dancers, it will make you "pull up" and your audition skills will improve. By the time you are 18, you will know many of the decision makers, and you will not be intimidated once you "officially" start going after the same job as the adults!

SECRETS OF THE AUDITION PROCESS

We're not going to lie to you, when we used to hold auditions for Michael and different artists, most of the dancers were already cast. We said we needed six dancers, but really we only needed one, because the other five were friends.

Sometimes, the choreographers already know who they want. In these cases, an audition is more for publicity for the choreographer and artist. Many auditions are not publicized to the public. If they are, the audition is publicity for a big artist like Madonna, Janet, or Michael Jackson to get support for their video or tour. Even for smaller, well-known artists, auditions are held to keep your name out amongst the world of dancers, agents, and other choreographers. "Hey, did you go to Tim's audition?" Auditions are also occasionally used as a marketing tool for the choreographer.

When you are auditioning for a dance job, be sure to have a *dance* resume and headshot. A choreographer does not want to see your choreography credits on your *dance* resume. (Choreographers tend to be a self-conscious bunch. Any threat to their job security will be vigorously defended!). Tim actually lost a dance job which would have taken him to Japan because he had choreography on his *dance* resume.

Tim auditioned for a choreographer and was killing it at the audition. People thought he knew the choreography the day before, because he was teaching people the steps outside the audition room. He was never called for the job. Several weeks after the audition, friends asked him how he liked Japan. He had to tell them that he didn't get a chance to go. On a random occasion, Tim ran into the choreographer for the Japan job. When he asked him why he was not chosen as one of the dancers, the choreographer told him that he did not get the job because he had choreography on his resume!

Can you believe that? Here is a choreographer who is admitting to him that he had insecurities! He was so insecure that he did not book Tim on a job because he was also a choreographer!

People; don't be fooled into believing that he is the only one with these insecurities. We would dare say that most choreographers feel the same way. Hollywood is a "What have you done for me lately?" kind of town; a place where you are only as good as your last project. The turnover is very high, and nothing is guaranteed. Unless a choreographer gets to the point where there is a contract stating that they are guaranteed work, or they do like other choreographers and give the director a kickback on their choreography pay or other "perks"; a job can be lost at anytime.

Make your life easy and be a dancer, not a dancer who wants to choreograph. (Or at least, don't let the choreographer know of your aspirations!)

CALLBACKS

Sometimes a choreographer needs to sift through a large number of dancers in order to find what they deem the best. These dancers are asked to come back and re-audition at a later time in order for the decision makers to view the crème de la crème. This is what is referred to as a callback.

When you are notified about a callback, you should keep a couple things in mind. The first is *do not* change your look for the callback, you want to make sure they see you as they did in the first audition.

The second thing is to remember the steps from the first audition in case they repeat it or add to it. Sometimes they will teach something completely new, or in some cases, a completely different style. For example, at the audition, the routine was hip-hop, but at the callbacks, its jazz, so be prepared. Don't be surprised if you get there and there is the same amount of dancers as the first call or even people who were not there at all. There is usually some casting going on in the background that you will not be aware of. Don't even worry about it, you are there to make your presence known and not to stress yourself out with the who's and what's.

Getting a callback is always good because it means you have already been noticed once and now you have increased your chances of booking the job. Keep in mind that if you make it to this stage, the choreographer, director, or producer knows you and your face! This is great, because they are more likely to remember you at the next audition if you do not land this job.

This is why we stress that you go to every audition. Don't expect that you will book every job. Your goal should be to land in the final group. What happens after that is no longer in your hands. Your look, the ratio of men to women, your ethnicity, your height, all come into play at this point. Don't worry about the things you can't change and be proud of the fact that you are in the conversation! Again, if you are 16 or 17 and attending auditions for adults, don't expect to book the job. Think of yourself as interning with a new corporation. You have to put in time, hard work, and effort before you will be noticed. But *when* you get noticed, your career will go through the roof once you turn 18, as long as you have talent, a good work ethic, and personality.

The more callbacks you get, the greater the percentage of jobs you will book. It's a numbers game! At the end of the callback, don't forget to shake hands with the choreographer, director, or casting agent, and tell them "Thank You!" Remember, you are *always* thinking about booking the next job!

Now that you know how to land a job, let's find out more about the people who will play an important role in your career.

CHAPTER FOUR

The Players in Your Career

For you to navigate through this business well, it's important for you to know the different players that can have an impact on your career. This could be from someone directly asking for you on their next project, having you choreograph their next project, or connecting you with other people who could help your career. They are:

AGENTS

Your agent is the most important person in your career. However, you need to be realistic on what an agent does and what they can do for you.

An Agent *CAN:*

> **Get you into auditions**. Your agent should have a good knowledge of your talent as a dancer and use that knowledge whenever an opportunity comes across his or her desk to either submit you on a project or call you on a particular audition. They can use their name and influence in order to try and get you opportunities. Though employers sometimes hold open auditions to cast dancers for jobs, most are closed, meaning you need an agent to grant you access.

> **Negotiate your pay and contract**. Keeping track of the business details of your dance career can be simple if you have a full-year contract with a company. However, commercial dancers often juggle dozens of shorter gigs a month. Once you book a job, your agent will handle the financial and legal aspects, like negotiating pay, making sure you're paid on time and approving contracts. For music tours, there are often 30- or 40-page contracts that dancers have to sign. Your agent is more than capable of looking over those contracts and trying to revise them if

possible. Your agent will make sure you're paid fairly, including overtime or double-time pay when needed and extra money when it's due—like if you're using your own wardrobe for a job, or working on a music video that will also be sold on iTunes.

An Agent *CANNOT*:

> Help you with your networking, marketing, audition skills, or navigate you through the politics of the industry. This is why we say that agents get 10% of the pay. It's because they do 10% of the work - the other 90% is left up to you.

CHOREOGRAPHERS

In all honesty, the real master-minds of the visual process in front of the camera are the choreographers. This is why they can command $1,500 to $3,500 a day for their services. As dancers who became choreographers, we have many experiences dealing with all of the politics that go into working with a Jamie King, Kenny Ortega, Adam Shankman, or a Fatima Robinson. While getting in good with a working choreographer is the best career move you can make, you will need to navigate this political area carefully in order to assure success (Politics page 103).

DANCERS

Taking class, going to auditions, booking jobs, you will come across the path of thousands of dancers. That being the case, you would be wise in making friends with as many of them as possible. Aside from having another ally in the business (which is always good), you should look at every person as your potential boss. Some of those dancers will become a director, a producer, a choreographer, or an actor. The entertainment world is small, and even if none of your immediate acquaintances graduate to a higher position of authority, they will no doubt know someone that has. You *always* want to be viewed as a positive, friendly, hard working, person in the industry; there are too many stripes against you to not be. Keeping your

Facebook and MySpace renewed with new faces that you meet daily will be a huge benefit for you.

DIRECTORS

The director is the person with much of the "vision" of the project you are working on. We like to think of a director as a choreographer with a camera, which is why some choreographers become directors. As you progress in your career, you will come across different directors with different styles. They set the tone on the set. Some of them are high strung, some are laid back, and some are all business. Your ability to not only deal with the different personalities and put yourself in a position where they will remember you for their next job, will be huge shot in the arm for your career.

PRODUCERS

The person who is responsible for making sure the project runs on time and under budget are the producers. Consider them the "money people". They are usually linked to the director, since many directors like to use the same producers, though this is not always the case. As with a Director, your ability to make yourself memorable so that they will think of you on their next job will help your career.

ACTORS/SINGERS

We decided to put both actors and singers on this list because we have personally had relationships with both that have helped our careers. As friends, they have personally advocated for us to book jobs on television shows and movies. Additionally, we both know dancers where their relationship has ended up in something unexpected, like a marriage. Now, we are not advocating dating between a dancer and actor or singer, we are simply saying that the relationship can lead to advantages, career wise, and as such, we wanted to mention that they could also play a part in your career.

MANAGERS

Manager will actively try to find jobs for you. Unlike an agent, they are not worried about sending you out on many calls in hopes that you land one. A good manager meticulously searches all avenues in order to find a job for you. This being the case, expect to pay 20% to a manager for their services. If you are just starting out, you do not need a manager. But once you are working fairly consistently, and you are looking to make the jump into bigger and better things such as acting, choreography, or singing, a manager could be crucial during this transitional phase in your life.

While this list describes the main people who you will come in contact with in the Hollywood dance industry, it's by no means the only group that could make a difference in your career. Others include casting agents, record company executives, television network executives, and executives from the product or service you are dancing for. The point is this: Be open, ready, and aware for any opportunity that comes your way. It may be closer than you think.

Now would be a good time to mention that the people above are smart, creative, and highly paid. They have connections that could help your dance career or help you move into some other realm in the entertainment business. Though that is the case, they are still only people. Don't be intimidated. They are usually very approachable and a great resource for knowledge. But how do you get into their circle, even if only temporarily while working on a job for them? Read on and find out.

CHAPTER FIVE

You Booked the Gig-Now What?

After the initial call and callback, you finally get the message that you've been waiting for all day.

You got the job!

After you get over your initial rush of excitement, you gather your thoughts and begin to ask your agent important questions. Where are rehearsals? What time? When is the shoot? Where is the location? Is there a fitting? How much money again? Now that all of your initial questions are answered (there will be more), it's time to think about what you can expect on the job, what to do if you are asked to choreograph a section, and what should you do when the job is wrapped. Figuring this part out will help ensure you leave a good first impression with everyone on the set, which could help you secure your next job. And, if you are lucky, provide you footage for your choreographic reel.

ARRIVE EARLY ON THE SET

Usually, shoot day is very stressful, so you coming in late will only lead to more stress- not good. The crew will have arrived hours before you, setting up lighting, props, and cameras. That team includes the players who will have a possible hand in future projects involving you. They are the wrong people to make angry by your tardiness.

After letting a production assistant know that you have arrived, ask for a *crew list*. This is a list with all the names and numbers of the people involved with the project. It is a very valuable tool and can be used to keep you connected with the important players such as the Director, Producer, or the Choreographer. *Note*: This list is gold and is not always readily available to a lowly dancer. Still, we highly suggest you find a way to get your paws on one! If the production team says that they are not giving them out, then be sure to keep your eyes open while on the set; someone is bound to misplace one.

Normally, you will meet the 1st Assistant Director, or 1st A.D. He or she is the one usually screaming at everyone to be quiet, or directing you to stand on your mark. Be sure to introduce yourself to them, as many 1st A.D.'s are aspiring directors.

If you are working on a music video, the *crew list* will also have the contact number of the representative(s) from the record company. This is gold! Be sure to introduce yourself to these people as well. If they like you, they may advocate for you on the next job involving dancers for the record company. Since you are going to be meeting so many people on the set, it would be a good idea to develop your observation skills, your communication skills, and your memory skills. During our seminar, we work on all three so that you will be able to present yourself in a professional manner, while at the same time, pumping the players for important information about future projects.

We cannot stress this enough: This business is about whom you know, not your skills as a dancer. The more information you know that others do not, the better your chances for getting yourself in line for the next project.

The star is the Star

No matter how good a dancer or performer you are, remember this: The star is the star.

You are a pawn, remember that. You will not be discovered on the set, so don't be singing or over acting. Typically, dancers are not treated the same as actors or models. After a long day of hurry up and wait, you will probably dance at the end of the day, in heels, and on wet cement. You may not get the attention you deserve from hair and make-up, so bring your own supplies.

Once when Courtney was on tour with Michael Jackson, he was performing "Smooth Criminal." He had friends in the audience that evening, so he would do small things so that they could pick him out of the other dancers on stage. During the dance, he got an extra shot of adrenaline during the famous lean. He bent over to the point where his nose was virtually inches from the floor. He went on to have a great show. Afterward, the dance captain came to him and said "Michael asks that you don't lean so far!" So, don't forget who the star is!

RAPPORT

Throughout the day, you should try and get to know everyone on set. But you want to get especially friendly with the Director, Producer, Choreographer, and any representative from the company responsible for paying for the shoot. This could be a record company representative, a corporation executive, or the manager of some actor or singer. These are people who you want to remember you when the next job comes up.

You will learn how to rapidly remember names and faces of people you work with. This comes in very handy on the set. Always listen to and follow the direction of the choreographer or director. Don't make them have to repeat the same thing twice. Find the right time to give a positive comment or appropriate joke to the players on the set. Laughter is a great way to build rapport with the important people.

Like many other jobs, there is a caste system on the set. The Director, Producer, Choreographer, and Company Representative are at the top of the food chain. This rings true during everyone's favorite time: lunch. During lunch, everyone sits in their own groups: electricians with electricians, make-up artists with make-up artists, actors with actors. But the table everyone wants to be at, is sitting with the top dogs. There are only a few seats, and if you've done what you are supposed to do, like arriving on time, having a positive attitude, and learning people's names, you might have a chance to sit at that table. You have left a hefty deposit in the rapport bank account, and the payoff is that at lunch, you will be able to sit at the table with the people who are planning their next job. Cha-Ching!

While at the table, you will hear a lot of gossip, rumor, and future job info. Your job is to shut up and listen. Speak up only when appropriate to show that you belong in the group, but don't try to dominate the conversation unless someone defers to you. Remember, this business is about who and what you know. Now that you have established rapport and eaten lunch with the decision makers, if you were not able to find out about upcoming projects before this, you still may have a chance! This is tricky because you will have to find the right time to ask this question. It could be at the end of lunch or at the end of the day, but this is everything you've been building up to. Ideally, you would ask each of the players separately, but understandably, you may not be able to get to each of them. Do what you can and be confident in the fact that some information is better than no information.

There is definitely a right way and wrong way to ask the question, "What job are you working on next?" Keep in mind that you can *only* do this if you were successful in establishing a rapport, able to sit during lunch, and were able to make the person you have targeted laugh (Yes, I said targeted). If so, feel free to ask away. N*ever* ask the person directly, *always* begin with some other topic. It could be something that was discussed at lunch, some current event, or you could give a commendation of some sort. Here are some examples:

"How many more days do you have to work on this project?" .Wait for a response. "I see. What's next up for you?"

"Seems like everything has gone pretty smooth today, huh?" Wait for a response. "After you finish with the edits, what's next for you?"

Keep it short and sweet. Show interest, wait for a response, acknowledge their statement, and ask your question.

The important point to remember is this: Never come out and ask, "What is your next project?" Make some sort of comment. A commendation coupled with a question always works. Don't think that people do not like sharing what their next project is. They love it!

People, especially in this business, love to talk about how great they are or what they've got going on. All you have to do is ask.

Always keep your eyes and ears open. There is always a "next job" and you want to be the person they remember when it comes time to shoot. Over the years, we have secured many jobs by working with the same director or producer over and over again. In fact, when you look at our dance and choreography resume, you will see the same names over and over again. This is because we were on someone's mind for the next job; you can do this, too. If you play the game correctly, you will find our advice keeps you on the mind of the decision makers.

CHOREOGRAPHY

After you have built a rapport with a choreographer, and they start to book you directly without the hassle of an audition, you may be asked to choreograph a section. When that happens, what should you do? Most of the time, you will receive neither credit nor compensation for helping. But if you say no, you may not work with the choreographer again. Hmmm. You're in a rock and a hard place.

If you are asked to choreograph a section by the choreographer, feel honored, knowing that this rite of passage, the stealing of choreography without receiving credit or pay, is as old as time. Actually, most everyone who is a currently a choreographer has gone through this process. Whether it is making up a structured, choreographed number in rehearsals or on the set, or freestyling in front of a camera at an audition, only to see those steps appear in the newest and hottest music video, stand tall and be proud of the fact that you are now in the inner circle of a small fraternity traveled by most aspiring choreographers.

If you do some choreography on a project, and you are not receiving pay or credit, be sure to get the name, number, and address of the production company. You need this information to not only send your thank you card to the producer and director, but you will want to get a copy of the project on DVD or Video Tape. No production company will give you a copy of the project prior to it being released to the general audience, so you may need to be a little patient.

Giving choreography away is different than having your steps stolen from you. One of the most common ways your choreography will be stolen is ironically during the time you are most vulnerable to get the job: the audition.

Freestyling at an audition is one of the ways choreography is stolen. The choreographer gets you on tape, and takes it home and studies you. In many cases, the steps are used, but the original creator of the step is not. One of the most marketed "How to Dance like a Celebrity" DVD's used steps that were not choreographed by the choreographer. It went on to sell 1.5 million copies. It happens.

"THAT'S A WRAP!"

After you are done with shooting your part, be sure to thank the Director, Producer, and 1ˢᵗ Assistant Director. Keep in mind that they may still be working, so be discreet if that is the case. Of course, thank the Choreographer for the opportunity, and at your earliest chance, send the Director and the Choreographer a thank you card. For the Director, send the card to the production company. For the Choreographer, send it to their agent- unless, of course, you have their address. If you took a photo with any of the players, include this with the card. If not, it's no big deal, the fact that you took time to send them a thank you note keeps you on their mind. Send this out no later than one week after the job is over. Remember, out of sight, out of mind. Don't add a phone number to your card. If they want to use you on the next job, they know how to find you or your agent.

Now that you finished the job, there is nothing to worry about right? Wrong. This is the time where many dancers join new circles of friends. The pressure to succeed triples now that they have had a taste of success. Now is the time we typically see increased drinking and drugs in newer dancers. However, this is the time where you really want to get a good handle on yourself by making sure you stay grounded.

CHAPTER SIX

Know Your Place

*W*hen you dance with some of the most famous singers, you get a chance to experience their world first hand. Photo shoots, interviews, hanging around other famous and powerful people. This opportunity is only presented to a select few! If they are lucky, a dancer will get the chance to be interviewed, on television, radio, or newspaper. In effect, you become a mini-star because you are in the right place at the right time with the right artist. You could even have your own fan-base. This can be intoxicating and could cause some to lose their frame of reference. Remember:

You are with the star, you are not the star.

Dancers are pseudo-stars. You dance next to the star, which can give some a big head, thinking they are a star when they are not. A former Britney Spears dancer once told us that many of the fans were not there to see Britney, but instead were there to see him. Now, let's think about this. In one corner, you have an amazing multi-platinum selling superstar who sells out 30,000 seat arenas consistently. In the other corner, you have a dancer getting paid $1,500 per week by the artist, and this dancer thinks the 30,000 tickets are being sold so that people can see him? His head got so big that he eventually stopped dancing for her, because he was going to pursue his career as a solo singing sensation. I'm still waiting for his album to come out.

In the audition chapter, we mentioned that your look was important. We stated that we knew of some choreographers who had overlooked some male dancers because their "look" was effeminate. Even if our Britney dancer-turned-singer had the most amazing pipes, he would be a hard sell to the public because his look was gay. Even in the 21st century, it's rare to find a new artist market themselves as gay. RuPaul was the exception, not the rule. It's ironic because the industry is very gay and bi-curious, but you cannot be out of the closet as a singer when you start. America is not ready for that quite yet.

The moral of this story is that you have to know your place as a dancer. You are backing up the artist. You are there to make *them* look good. You will quickly burn bridges if you start acting like a superstar while working for someone else. If you want to be the star, then do like Jennifer Lopez did when she left Janet Jackson's tour, just do it.

THE PRESSURE OF THE BUSINESS

When people ask us about the business, one of the first things we tell them is that you have to have the stomach for rejection. You will be told "no" very often. Even if you book half the jobs you audition for, you're still told no 50% of the time. It's a tough world out there, and in this industry you will we be shot down, stepped on, and talked about. We have one rule for ourselves and one rule that we think everyone should abide by: "It doesn't mean anything, because there's only one of you." You can be your worst critic. You may be constantly second guessing yourself and asking yourself whether or not this business is for you. But, if you work on your craft and put your heart and soul into it, there is a place for you in this business. Never let anyone tell you different. We have had people tell us that we would not be able to dance on MTV because it's so competitive. When they saw us dancing with Jennifer Lopez, Michael Jackson or Beyoncè, they were floored. You can make it in this industry; you just have to work hard in order to reach your goal. There are hundreds of great dancers, but there's only one of you and you have to remember that your biggest competition is yourself. The pressure of the business will always be there; you can't do anything about it, so learn to push through it.

KEEPING YOUR DIGNITY

Temptations, broken promises, and lies are all a part of this business. This is important to understand at the beginning of your career. We love dance, that's why we do it. That's why we trained for so long. That's why we spent countless hours in class, danced in free shows, and spent all that time in rehearsals. When you begin to take your career seriously by thinking of the business side of dance, remember not to lose your dignity. Don't get lost in the dark side of the business and give up your soul for any job. There are many amazing people in the industry, and there are also some losers. People can be your ally to help you get where you want to go, but there are those who will try and use you to get where they want.

Stand up for what your heart believes in and don't let the eagerness of wanting to work weaken your ability to keep your dignity. It's not worth the issues that may spring forth, nor the regret that could come later. Always be the bigger person and always stand your ground, because the players in the business who matter have more respect for individuals who are not backstabbing, and instead are honest, respectful, and true. There was a situation where Tim was dancing on the last leg of a world tour. The member of the management company asked the dancers to work for free, citing the performance was supposed to be for the troops in Germany. The company assumed that by using the "We are doing this for the troops" statement, they could get around from paying the dancers, even though the artist he was dancing for was getting paid!

But like we say, do your research. After asking around, he found out that another artist had just left the same show during a previous month and had paid her dancers $1,200 each for that week. He wasn't willing to let someone take advantage of the situation, while millions was being paid to the artist. He explained to the production company that since they were willing to assure the artist got paid, but not the dancers, he would like to be sent home. When the artist heard about the situation, Tim was informed that the dancers would get full pay for the week and that he and another dancer were the ones she appreciated the most, because they had stood their ground.

It's important to remember that the industry can be fun, exciting, and memorable. At the same time, remember that it is a high stakes business and big money sometimes draws bad people. Be aware of who you are as a person. This means your morals, your integrity, and your limitations.

Remember that you are dancing with the star, you are not the star. Be wise with your money, remembering the fact that the great job you are working on now will not be there forever, and at some point, you will have to find another job. People will make promises that they can't keep. Be aware of this from the beginning. One of the promises that they will make has to do with the amount of pay you could make on a job. It's important that you arm yourself with the knowledge of what you could typically expect as compensation from one job to the next. The next chapter talks about pay in greater detail.

CHAPTER SEVEN

PAY

*T*he pay for dancers varies greatly based on the type of project (music video, live show, or commercial), how many days you are working on the job, and(in the case of television) whether you are performing as a solo artist or in a group.

A good dancer can average about $54,000 a year, working on one music video a week every week of the year (that's two rehearsal days and one shoot day). Not bad, but not earth shattering. This is why it is important that your look allows you to get involved with other facets of the entertainment business. You make the most money by far with commercials, and you can make a great living by dancing on tour as well.

When Courtney danced on his first tour with En Vogue, he made $500 a week. That's $2,000 a month, $24,000 a year. It didn't matter. He was 19, fresh out of high school, and he wanted to go on tour so bad, he didn't care about the rate. Everything from his flights, hotel, and food were paid for. He was performing with the hottest girl group in the world. He was staying in the same hotel as the artists and experiencing the same public events with them.

When he danced for Michael on the History Tour, he made $2,200. That's $8,800 a month, $105,600 a year, somewhat of an upgrade. However, not everyone pays like Michael. You would be lucky to get $1,000 - $1,500 these days.

There is no set fee a dancer can make on a tour. It depends on the budget they have put together for dancers. A large part of that is based on who the artist is. An example of the huge difference between rates based upon the artist is Carmen Electra. A former rapper, Electra was signed on Prince's label, and was a damn good dancer. When we went on tour with Carmen, we were making $800 a week performing 3 songs in a show. Compare that to the $500 from En Vogue and the

$2200 from Michael Jackson and you can see that rates are all over the place. Still, tours are nice, because they provide a steady weekly paycheck.

You can have variations in pay and duration of time before you see your paycheck for a television show appearance. Expect three to four weeks before you see a paycheck. For union jobs, if the show incorporates several dancers, the rate for all dancers will be lowered. This is what happened on a Disney job Courtney was choreographing. In fact, his desire to hire more dancers than budgeted for caused a rift between he and a dance agent.

Initially, 16 dancers were budgeted for the job. At the audition, there were four phenomenal dancers who, by their dancing and attitude, changed his mind and the dancer total. He had to have them! So, he asked if the budget could be amended to add four additional dancers, for a total of 20. Due to the fact that these dancers were not budgeted, the rate for every dancer was lower. Somehow, this information got back to their agent, who called Courtney cursing and yelling. The agent was demanding that Courtney stick to the Dancer's Alliance rate. The conversation that ensued during the middle of rehearsal was a classic reason as to the benefits of having an agent.

Agent: "How the hell can you hire dancers beneath the Dancer's Alliance rate?"
Courtney: "What the &*%$ are you yelling for? I'm hiring additional dancers outside of budget; they should be happy to have a job!"
Agent: "By not sticking to the rate, you are hurting the dance community!"
Courtney: "Don't even try to $%&*#$ come at me, because I know for a fact you have your choreographers hold closed auditions for dancers from your agency and offer the production company lower rates if they use only your dancers!"

If the dancers and choreographer all came from the same agency, it will allow the agency to make more money than they would with only a couple of the agency's dancers booking the job. We were on the phone during rehearsal for about 30 minutes. As the situation grew tense, Courtney could see that many of the dancers represented by the agency were afraid that he was going to fire them. Courtney would have done exactly that, but the agency accepted the terms of the deal.

It seems a couple of the dancers had been complaining about the rates. We don't mind if a dancer has a price they will not dance for. But don't take the job knowing the rates in the beginning, and then complain about them. The rates were $50 less than the norm. Instead of $250 per rehearsal, they got $200. Can you work making $50 less? That's a choice you have to make as an individual. If you're smart, you'll keep in mind that you would make money for the next 5 years on residuals, because Disney would play the hell out of that episode. Courtney danced on an episode of *That's So Raven* and still gets checks, four years after the fact. There are a lot of dancers that audition for each job, and if you don't want the money, someone else does. Complaining about the rate after you book the job is a good way to never work for that choreographer again. Ultimately, money is king.

Here is how much you can make as a dancer, according to the rates set forward by Dancer's Alliance (a dance organization) and SAG (the Screen Actors Guild). Keep in mind, these rates change annually.

Music Video
Paid in 30 days

Rates

Rehearsal
$250 for an 8 hour day
$175 for a 4 hour day
After 8 hours, overtime is time-and-a-half

Fittings
$50 if not on rehearsal day

Shoot day
$550 for 12 hours

Tours
Paid weekly

Rates

Rehearsal
Half the agreed-upon weekly salary.

On-Road / Off-Road
Some contracts are set up with an ON-ROAD and OFF-ROAD rate (For an example of this, see Courtney's contract with Michael Jackson.).

Salary
From $1000 - $2500 per week

Industrials
Paid in 30 days

Rates

Rehearsal
$350 for an 8 hour day

Show Day
$350 for an 8 hour day

Commercial / Television
Paid in 30 days

Rates

Daily Rate
$782 solo/duo dancers
$685 three to eight dancers
(See why we like commercials so much?)

Weekly rate
$2,513 solo/duo
$2,303 three to eight
*per SAG (Screen Actors Guild)

The above list is what is typical for a dancer in Hollywood. Whether your job is for a film, television show, industrial, or concert; the rates above are in the ballpark of what you can expect.

On the next page is a standard contract for going on tour with an artist. In this case, we chose to use Courtney's contract when he went on tour with Michael Jackson.

ULTIMATE TOUR PRODUCTIONS, LLC ("Producer")
c/o Ziffren, Brittenham, Branca & Fischer
2121 Avenue of the Stars
32nd Floor
Los Angeles, California 90067

EMPLOYMENT DEAL MEMORANDUM

	DATE: June 12, 1996
NAME: COURTNEY MILLER	START DATE: June 7, 1996
("Employee")	POSITION: Dancer
ADDRESS:	DUTIES: All customary duties of
	a dancer.

HOME PHONE: _____
SERVICE: (___) _____
S.S: _____
W-4 EXEMPTIONS: _____
UNION LOCAL: _____

COMPENSATION PER WEEK:
"ON-ROAD": $ 2,200
"OFF-ROAD": $ 1,650

This Employment Deal Memorandum shall be subject to Producer's Standard Terms and Conditions attached hereto and incorporated herein by this reference.

This Employment Deal Memorandum, the Producer's Standard Terms and Conditions and any executed Rider to Employment Agreement attached hereto (if any) shall constitute our full agreement unless amended or modified in writing and signed by the parties hereto.

"PRODUCER"
ULTIMATE TOUR PRODUCTIONS, LLC

Date:_____

By_____
Its Authorized Signatory

"EMPLOYEE"

Date:_____

_____
COURTNEY MILLER

TO: All Individuals Hired by Ultimate Tour Productions, LLC
              To Perform Services In Connection With The Michael Jackson
              Concert in Brunei on July 16, 1996 And The Michael Jackson
              HIStory World Tour Commencing Approximately September 7, 1996

FROM: Management

RE: Hotel Incidentals

Please be advised that all individuals hired by Ultimate Tour Productions, LLC to perform services in connection with the Michael Jackson concert in Brunei on July 16, 1996 and/or the Michael Jackson HIStory World Tour commencing approximately September 7, 1996 will be responsible for their incidental hotel charges. Incidental hotel charges include, without limitation, hotel charges billed to your room relating to use of the telephone, room service, restaurant meals, gift shop purchases, personal services offered by the hotel, hotel facility charges (e.g., pool, fitness center, etc.), and mini-bar bills. All such charges must be paid directly to the hotel by you on or before check-out time. In the event you fail to comply with this policy, Ultimate Tour Productions, LLC will deduct in full from your following week's paycheck any such incidental hotel charges you have incurred.

ACKNOWLEDGMENT AND AUTHORIZATION

I have read the foregoing policy and understand that it is my responsibility to pay for all incidental hotel charges I incur during the time I am working on the Michael Jackson concert in Brunei on July 16, 1996 and/or the Michael Jackson HIStory World Tour. I understand that incidental expenses include, without limitation, hotel charges billed to my room relating to use of the telephone, room service, restaurant meals, gift shop purchases, personal services offered by the hotel, hotel facility charges (e.g., pool, fitness center, etc.) and min-bar bills. I further understand that any such incidental bills which I have failed to pay prior to leaving the hotel will be automatically deducted in full from my following week's paycheck, and I hereby authorize Ultimate Tour Productions, LLC to make such deductions.

_____
COURTNEY MILLER

Date: _____

Now that you have a good idea as to the amount of money you can make dancing, let's turn our attention to how you can better market yourself, so that you are in a better position to land these jobs.

CHAPTER EIGHT

MARKETING YOURSELF

*I*t's so important to market oneself. Think about the choreographers that you can rattle off the top of your head. There are many good choreographers, but only a few work consistently because they are good at marketing themselves. They may not have the most memorable or the most phenomenal steps, but you know who they are. You recognize their name because of their ability to get their name into the public. Shane Sparks, celebrity judge of the hit show "America's Best Dance Crew," once said in an interview with Popmatters.com, that, he believes that "dancers need to market themselves in the same way that other entertainers and athletes have for years."

Talking about first season winners of "America's Best Dance Crew," he says "the Jabbawockeez are a smart crew. If they're really smart, they'll get out there and market themselves so well that they get that... million dollar deal for wearing Nike stuff. Just like [how] Tiger Woods gets out there and puts on a Nike shirt, to swing at a ball. They get out there and spin on their heads, jump off stage, spitting fire, doing this and doing that, breaking their backs. They should get the same respect." Marketing yourself as an amazing dancer is no different than what is done to market a new actor or singer. Obviously you don't have millions of dollars being used to push you and your name out into the public, but there are many things you can do to promote, sale, and distribute your brand into the dance community. In order for a dancer to be successful at marketing themselves, it's important that they have a clear understanding of what marketing is, what means are available to market themselves, and the benefits of marketing.

To begin with, let's define marketing. Marketing is:

The commercial processes involved in promoting and selling and distributing a product or service.

In this case, that product is you and the service is your ability to dance. Distribution of your ability can come via the internet or in person during dance class. Let's break this sentence down into three main areas: Promoting, Selling, and Distributing.

PROMOTING

Promoting is simply getting the word out about something or someone. To put it plainly, it's advertising. For a dancer, advertising takes many shapes and forms. Its how you dress, how you talk, how you dance- basically, everything about you. You are always promoting yourself, whether you say something or not. Of course, as the saying goes; "Actions speak louder than words." Much of your self-promoting will come through your dancing, which is why taking class with working choreographers at places like the Edge and the Millennium Dance Complex can be a great way to "promote" your skills as a dancer to these decision makers. (Just make sure to have an extra headshot and resume in the car).

Some other things to consider when taking class at these well-known facilities:

1. **Every class is an audition**. The teacher may be a choreographer and will base their decision about you from their experience in class. You have the advantage of them knowing you in class, as the teacher knows you know their style and they have the benefit of experiencing your work ethic. Many close friends of ours who are well-known choreographers will do straight booking with students from class because they have a rapport with those dancers. We've booked people who took class from us for Disney television, music videos, and live concerts, instead of going through the audition process if time was a factor.

2. **Play nice with your classmates.** Other dancers in class may also be on the road to being a choreographer and they will also use the experience they had with you in class against you or for you. They will also recommend you for a job to other people if they like you if someone asks them about other good dancers they know. Be cordial to everyone. You never know who you are talking to or standing next to in class.

3. **You never know who may drop in**. Directors, dance agents, choreographers and casting agents have been known to drop by studio classes just to see who the new people are, and who's been killing it in class.

Besides dancing in class, there are many other ways to promote yourself. Technology had made this very easy and basically free. Twitter, Facebook, YouTube, and MySpace have allowed dancers to post their most recent photos, tell people what they are working on and send videos to everyone to show off their work. The great thing about all of this is you have the ability to change and update daily. It's really easy to use and you can have a large audience. As word gets around about your dancing, many choreographers will hear about you as well. This can be a benefit for you when you audition for these choreographers, as they will already be familiar with you and your work. Another benefit about these sites is that you can use one to support the other. For example, your YouTube video can show on YouTube, MySpace, and Facebook. Again, this is a great way to promote yourself for free and generate a little buzz about you. Many of you use those sites everyday anyway; you might as well start utilizing them for your career.

Once you generate a following of your other social network accounts, you can use twitter by tweeting short amounts of information in order to:

1. **Direct traffic**. Twitter can be used to get traffic to your website (including your MySpace) or the sites of friends. If you ask your friends to tweet about it, the message will spread faster and further as other active users pick it up. There is a viral nature to all types of news, even on a site like Twitter.
2. **Networking**. Like any other social network, Twitter has a built-in function for you to befriend and track the messages of other users. This is an easy way for you connect with people outside of your usual circle. Make an effort to add active users you find interesting. A Twitter acquaintance can be developed into a business contact.
3. **Event Updates**. A dancer can use Twitter as a means to inform followers of the latest event happenings/changes. Perfect for when you are in rehearsal or on the set doing a job!

4. **Provide live coverage**. Twitter's message size limit prevents detailed coverage of events but it can allow you to provide real-time commentary which may help to spark further discussion or interest on the event as other Twitter users spread the message. Great if you are on tour or performing during a live show.

We would suggest using Twitter as way to promote yourself and conduct research. You can look for choreographers, producers, and directors on the site in order to keep up with what they are working on. This info will be useful as a conversation starter when you meet them face to face.

MySpace can be used as your own personal website. If you have a MySpace or will be setting one up, be sure to utilize the personalized name function. This makes it much easier for individuals to find you. With MySpace, you can upload photos and video along with other fun applications.

Facebook is slowly taking the place of MySpace as a personal website. At this point, it would be good to have both. It's important to update them daily so that your followers will have something to look forward to.

SELLING

The selling of your services comes two-fold. First, you attend an audition for a dance job where you dance in front a choreographer, casting agent, or a director. Here, you are selling them on your ability to sell the story or message they are trying to convey. The second way you sell your services comes when you are looking for dance related jobs such as teaching, judging, or choreographing, while you wait for your next audition.

By utilizing the websites and services of MySpace, Facebook, and YouTube, you can point potential hiring businesses to a venue with more information about you. For example; if you want to teach at a dance studio for consistent money while you await your next audition, it's great to not only provide the studio a photo and resume, but you can point them to your MySpace, Facebook, and YouTube pages as well, as a way to give yourself additional credibility.

DISTRIBUTING

Distribution can take place through various channels. We have been mainly focusing on using the internet as a way to promote, sell, and distribute your services, but with a little courage, persistence, and creativity, you could also promote yourself through your local newspaper, television station, and radio station, to get the message out about you.

A great way we utilize these sources are by contacting them when we know we are going to be traveling to another city or state for a speaking engagement, choreography job, or book signing. We make it a point to find out the names and contact information of the largest newspaper, television, and radio stations in those cities. If you can't find out who they are, ask a friend who lives in that area. We then call and ask to speak to the person in charge of entertainment reporting and explain who we are, why we are coming to the city, and how long we are going to be there. We ask if the newspaper or television station would like to come down to see the class and conduct an interview. You need to ask these things because this is how you are going to get these entities to distribute the message.

As a way to seal the deal, we send a press kit which contains:

> ➢ A press release about the upcoming event we are going to be taking part in.

> ➢ A photo, bio, resume and DVD of our choreography.

> ➢ Some magazine and newspaper clippings from previous interviews.

All of our information contains website (MySpace, Twitter, and Facebook) information that they can use as research prior to the interview. Once you get your first interview, the others come a little easier.

We do the same process for the local radio station. This does so much for promoting yourself and the event you are going to be attending. Even if you do not increase the number of people who attend the workshop, master class, or in our case, book signing, you still received free promotion for yourself. Be sure to get the contact information of the person or people involved in the interview. You want to get a copy of the article or television interview, so that you can add to your press kit for future use.

By marketing yourself, you are creating name recognition. This is so helpful for jobs in front of and off camera. This will make it much easier for you to earn a living during the "slow" times of the year when not much is happening in Hollywood. While your friends are telling you about the difficulty of the industry, you can be traveling all across the globe, teaching master classes, being a judge, or creating choreography for some artist in another country.

REALITY TV

This has been a huge asset for dancers in the past five years and is definitely a way to get exposure. Shows like *So You Think You Can Dance, America's Best Dance Crew, Dancing with The Stars, America's Got Talent* and more have paved the way for dancers to get a bigger audience and propel their career into another level. It helps them get noticed by casting directors, they get to work with some of the industry's top choreographers, and it will also secure great paying teaching and appearance jobs as well. In order to take full advantage of this opportunity, it is important to promote yourself while your name is hot and in the public. You may need to enlist the help of your agent, a publicist, or a creative and persistent friend in an effort to get your name out into the public so that you can secure jobs.

These shows serve as both promoting and distribution, but what many of the contestants fail to sell their services. All of their life they have wanted to be a dancer. They have focused on the creative side by taking class, going to auditions, and performing. Now, they are on a stage in front of millions, however, only a few of them think about what business opportunities lie in front of them after the show is over. This is why so many of the dancers from these shows fall into obscurity. Here is where a good mentor or agent can be of service. Enjoy the moment while you are in it, but remember, at some point it will end, so always think about what is next.

If you are fortunate enough to be among the top finalists in one of these shows, you should have the ability to set up great opportunities as a dancer, guest speaker, or choreographer when you are done. This can be done by your agent, a creative friend, or you could contact us for assistance. As I write this, I sent a text message to one of the contestants on *So You Think You Can Dance* who performed last night. He had been getting a verbal beat down from one of the judges who told him that the only reason why he was not in the bottom was because the girls liked him! Sobering, but a good reason to "pull up" the next time he performed. The next night, he did an amazing job on his solo. So I sent him this text:
"U r doin a gd job. Kp ur head up :) stay hmble dnt get a bad rep 4 bein cocky. Im proud of u. P.s. Evn if u r the best let ur dnce do the tlkng. kill it!"

I got a :) back. Later, as the season draws to an end, we will discuss how he can market himself for upcoming projects including choreography, master classes, and workshops.

This is what you need to do as a dancer. Set consistent goals and work toward them, knowing that at some point you will not be dancing in front of the camera.

What should you do in order to earn money when not performing on the stage or screen? Turn the page for a few suggestions.

CHAPTER NINE

BETWEEN JOBS

You will find out real quick that one job does not an income make. It's not always easy to have a steady income when you're hustling for work every week. If you have dry spells, you will need to have some supplemental income so that you can pay your bills and not starve. We had friends that were constantly couch-surfing and living like gypsies because they refused to get a job in hopes that they would always be booking jobs. The reality is that only a small percentage of dancers have that luxury and the rest go through the ups and downs.

When Tim was in the thick of auditioning and working, he found a couple jobs that could provide a somewhat steady stream of income, and flexibility in schedule for the occasions when he needed time off to work in front of the camera.

The first was teaching dance classes. This works because you can make 25 to 50 bucks per class, and when you have an audition, you can get a sub and not lose your job. When you book a job and promote yourself on Facebook, MySpace, and Twitter, you can actually increase your class sizes, making the studio owner happy. Of course, you can take the opportunity to make yourself happy as well, because increased class size is more money for both the studio and you!

The second job that really helped during the slow times was working for entertainment companies that used dancers for weddings, bar mitzvahs, graduation parties, and special events. These jobs were amazing because you are getting paid to dance and have a good time while making about 160 dollars or more for a 4 to 5 hour time period. It is possible to work two to three of these every weekend and it frees up time during the week for auditioning.

Some people will take up cocktail or waiting jobs, which can also work, but most of them have a little trouble covering shifts when they were booked on a job.

While it would be impossible to include every job a dancer can do between auditions, we wanted to give you a few ideas:

> **Judging for dance competitions**. If your weekends are free, and you are okay with traveling, you can submit your head shot and resume to dance competitions as a judge.

> **Master classes**. After putting together your press kit, contact dance studios, especially in the summer and winter. They typically host master classes to keep enrollment high during those months.

> **Workshops**. This is where your speaking, networking, and sales skills come in. You would need to contact dance studios, schools, and other arts facilities to conduct and promote your workshop. Or, you can get together with other dance friends and put the workshop on yourself.

> **Dancing for Disney**. You can work for The happiest place on earth on part-time bases. This will provide some stability, medical and dental benefits, and a means to make money when it is slow.

> **Starting your own business**. If you are entrepreneurial, you can start a side business. An amazing friend of ours sells baked desserts as his side job.

> As a last resort; and we do mean a last resort, you can **file for unemployment** and collect an unemployment check between jobs. However, you must remember to inform the unemployment office if you book a job, otherwise you will be "double-dipping" and this will have tax implications you don't want to get involved in.

Of course the goal is to work often enough, where you will not need to take many jobs on the side. If you work on television, stage, or in a movie, you will eventually need to join a union. How much are they to join? What are the bi-annual payments? How many unions are there? The next chapter discusses these questions.

CHAPTER TEN

UNIONS

*I*n your career, you will eventually need to join a union. This is true especially if you are doing a commercial, a movie, or live television show. Below is a list of the common unions, their costs, and website information. We need to be frank and let you know that currently, there is no dancer's union. The protections that dancer's enjoy come mainly as an extension of what is enjoyed by actors. As dance becomes more and more mainstream, we will see increased protections and hopefully the creation of a strong union. But that will be up to you!

SAG

Screen Actors Guild is the nation's largest labor union representing working actors. (SAG.org)

Established in 1933, SAG has a rich history in the American labor movement, from standing up to studios to break long-term engagement contracts in the 1940s to fighting for artists' rights amid the digital revolution sweeping the entertainment industry in the 21st century.

Cost to join: $2,277.00 (one-time fee - payment plan available)

Minimum Dues: $58 per dues period. Dues are billed twice a year, May 1st and November 1st. Fees may be lower if you join or work in a branch area other than Hollywood.

Website:
www.sag.org

AFTRA

The American Federation of Television and Radio Artists (AFTRA) is a national labor union that represents all professional performers working in recorded TV and Radio. AFTRA members are actors, announcers, singers, dancers, narrators as well as television and radio station personnel (reporters, writers, disc jockeys).

The union covers: Radio commercials; Television commercials (shot on video tape); Network TV; Audio cassettes and CD's; Network Cable; Educational TV and Radio; Interactive TV; Commercials for the Internet. (AFTRA.org)

Cost to join: $1,600.00 (one-time fee - payment plan available) Minimum Dues: $63.90 per dues period. Dues are billed twice a year, May 1st and November 1st.

Website:
www.aftra.org

Equity

Actors' Equity Association ("AEA" or "Equity"), founded in 1913, is the labor union that represents more than 48,000 Actors and Stage Managers in the United States. Equity seeks to advance, promote and foster the art of live theatre as an essential component of our society. Equity negotiates wages and working conditions and provides a wide range of benefits, including health and pension plans, for its members. Actors' Equity is a member of the AFL-CIO, and is affiliated with FIA, an international organization of performing arts unions. (actorsequity.org)

Cost to join: $1,100.00 (one-time fee - payment plan available) Minimum Dues: $59.00 per dues period. Dues are billed twice a year, May 31st and November 30th.

Website:
www.actorsequity.org

Dancer's Alliance

Dancers' Alliance is an organization created by dancers to standardize non-union work. D.A. rates are minimums imposed by dancers and agents to protect dancers' wages and working conditions that are not covered by union jurisdiction. D.A. is not a union! These rates are most effective and attainable if dancers know them and make an effort to attain them on every job. You don't need to have representation to apply these rates to your work.(Dancersalliance.org)

Dancer's Alliance is a guideline. Dancers are one of the few groups in entertainment who don't have a real union.

There are rates the organization asks production companies and choreographers to abide by. However, since the Alliance does not have any teeth (mainly because we as dancers do not stick together on rates), the pay for jobs can fluctuate widely from $50 a day for a music video rehearsal (although this is rare), to $300 a day (depending on the project).

Cost to join: $0
Minimum Dues: None

Website:
www.dancersalliance.org

AGVA

American Guild of Variety Artists (AGVA) is an American entertainment union representing performers in variety entertainment, including circuses, Las Vegas showrooms and cabarets, comedy showcases, dance revues, magic shows, theme park shows, and arena and auditorium extravaganzas. It awards the "Georgie Award" (after George Jessel) for Variety Performer of the Year. There is some overlap between the jurisdictions of AGVA and Actors' Equity.

Its office is in New York City. (agvausa.com)

Cost to join: $750 (one-time fee - payment plan available)
Minimum Dues: $24 per dues period. Dues are billed three times a year, April 1st, August 1st, and December 1st.

Website:
www.agvausa.com

CHAPTER ELEVEN

POLITCS of the BUSINESS

*P*olitics plays a huge role in your career as a dancer. Your ability to judge, navigate, and act upon this dynamic will either make or break your career. Next to your look and talent, politics is *the* most important part of a dancer's career. You will be faced with some hard decisions while in show business. Some of these choices you may not agree with completely. Our advice is to try to work within the system without selling your soul.

This chapter will talk about several controversial topics, including, drugs, sex, and manipulation in the Hollywood dance industry. We have put together some rules that you should follow in order to keep your wits and to help you navigate this industry unscathed.

Don't take anything you see or hear personally.

It's only business. This business only cares about the latest greatest thing, and that may not be you. What you don't know is that after you audition, someone may be advocating for you behind the scenes. But because you are not the right color, ethnicity, height, or weight, you may lose a job. We both were involved with the same job that caused us to fall victim to these behind-the-scenes politics.

At the time, Courtney was in New York as one of three choreographers creating the steps for Michael Jackson's "Dangerous" performance on the MTV Awards. He needed to replace a dancer who we had fired due to his bad attitude, and Courtney suggested Tim. His fellow choreographers balked at the idea because he was straight and they enjoyed having men around whom they could sleep with. Courtney told them, "Screw that, he can dance his butt off and you do want the number to be hot, don't you?" They reluctantly agreed and later that day, he took a flight back to Los Angeles in order to teach Tim the steps. Courtney rehearsed with him for three days in order to get Tim up to speed. Tim knew most of the choreography, because Courtney had already been feeding him the steps before he left for New York. (See how it's all about who you know?) After the third day, Courtney headed back to New York to join the rest of the group. He assured Tim that he would send for him, and to keep his phone ready at all times. When Courtney got back to the job, he was quickly brought up to speed on what he had missed and continued working on the job.

After the first day, Tim didn't show. Same thing on the second day, and the third. Still no Tim. Courtney had assumed that something had changed and that we did not need him any longer. Surely someone had called Tim's agent and explained the situation to him. Not only was Tim not contacted, but later Courtney found out that he was never brought in because he was not gay. This decision was never discussed or approved with Courtney, nor did we find out about what happened until after the job- it was all politics! As luck would have it, Michael fainted during rehearsal, and the show was cancelled.

Sex

As you can see from the previous story, a dancer will have to negotiate through sex and the gay – straight dynamic. Let's face it, dancers are sexy. The combination of hot bodies, limited jobs, and opportunity, makes for a sexual cocktail that one needs to prep themselves for. Men, whether gay or straight, will use their authority and promise opportunity, if you sleep with them. Men, if you are easily disturbed by a gay man propositioning you because you are straight, you may want to find another career. On the other hand, a beautiful woman needs to understand that many men will ask for sex in order to secure jobs. Or if you do book a gig, it may be that the choreographer is looking for sex as a way to show your "appreciation." While it is true that some women in authority will ask for sex from either men or women, it is far more prevalent the other way around. Most men would not mind having sex with the female choreographer, so we did not include that scenario here. But again, it does happen once in a while.

In addition to the choreographer, you have other dancers, the director, producer, casting agent, actors, and singers that may seek your company. We know of several female dancers who have slept with married (and unmarried) actors, singers, or musicians in order to either advance their career or hoping that the relationship would somehow becomes serious. Dance is a perfect gateway career to acting or singing, because you meet interesting, rich and famous people, while you move your body around. It has led many individuals to higher endeavors, including becoming a choreographer, director, leading actress, or a rich spouse. So don't be surprised if someone propositions you.

We can't tell you how many times we have been propositioned. In Courtney's case, it started when he was around 18. He was the new kid on the scene, and was seen as "fresh meat." He was at an audition where he had absolutely killed it. Being a boy among men, he stood out like a sore thumb. After making the first and second cuts, he was called in for the final group. There was a dancer with the same last name as his (Miller), who seemed to be a nice guy. After the audition, he told Courtney about a get-together he was having at his house, and asked if Courtney wanted to go. Thinking nothing of it, Courtney told him sure and went to his house for the party a couple of days later. The host met Courtney at the door with a glass of wine in hand and offered him some. Courtney responded that he would take some soda instead. Though he did a good job in delaying the advance by telling the host no wine, he did go to the party by himself. This was pre-GHB or any other, similar drug that could knock you out, but it was still a possible mistake. Courtney noticed several other dancers, guys and girls that he had seen on television in music videos and award shows as he was growing up. It was a regular *Who's Who* of some of the best in the business. He did not know anyone there, but he was comfortable with crowds and introducing myself to new people, so in no time, he had learned the names of most of the people at the party and found out that they had common friends or took class from the same teachers. After about an hour of meeting people, the host approached him for the "tour". Did we forget to tell you this was a 2-bedroom apartment the host shared with his "roommate"? Courtney saw the living room when he walked in; the kitchen was right in front of him, just off the living room. There really wasn't much to see. But, being oblivious, Courtney went along. He went to the guest bedroom, and then the *piece de resistánce:* he was lead to the master bedroom where the host's "roommate" sat on the bed, welcoming him in. Courtney quickly put two and two together and counted 3. Yep, they were hoping for a little *ménage* with the new buck in town! Courtney did a quick exit stage left!

The Hollywood dance scene can be compared to your local high school where you have different groups or cliques.

There are:

The **"cool kids"** – The consistently working dancer.

The **"tweakers"** – A dancer who books every once in a while. Their major focus is scoring weed.

The **"cheerleaders"** – Dancers who are moving into the realm of acting, commercials, and modeling.

The **"nerds"** – Dancers who never work. They were the best dancer in their high school or dance studio but can't seem to land a dance job in Hollywood.

In life as in show business, it's all about who you know. And that means getting in with the right clique. Once you get a label, it's hard to remove it. In our seminars, we break this down in more detail by role-playing some possible situations you may find yourself in. We discuss in great detail how to avoid putting yourself in a precarious situation, and we show you the way out if you do find yourself faced with a dilemma. Lastly, we show you how to use each experience as a learning tool to advance your career! We are going to help you navigate the Hollywood dance scene, so that you are in the right cliques to help your career.

Drugs

Let's take a moment to talk about drugs. Here's the thing, don't do them. Doing drugs isn't going to help you book work, and it's truly not respectful of the body you've worked hard to make sure was in top shape. Your focus needs to be on booking work and being a great dancer. But if you make the decision to engage in drug use, do them with someone who could help your career. Hanging out with unemployed dancers in your apartment, doesn't do much to help you book that next world tour. But recreational use with a top choreographer, director, producer, or casting agent, may create a relationship with them that could add years and money to your career. However, be warned that it could create the wrong kind of relationship with them. We're definitely not advocating drug use, but if you are going to do them for pleasure, do them around or with people who matter and can help you advance your career. You're an adult, so you're going to have to make these kinds of difficult choices. But we have both enjoyed successful careers in this industry without the use of drugs.

Some choreographers are manipulative, or may test you to see what they can get away with. Tim was new to the business. On the way to a club in New York with a big celebrity and her choreographer, they kept whispering and giggling back and forth with each other. Then the choreographer says, "I will do it if Tim does it." Tim said, "What are you talking about?" Now at this point in his life, he had never seen cocaine. He simply wasn't interested. In order to avoid the pressure to use cocaine, Tim said; "Give me a beer instead." Later, the limo arrived at the club. Everyone got out and was ushered into the V.I.P. section. Inside the club, the manipulation didn't stop. While there, the choreographer tried to get Tim to kiss a drag queen. Tim sternly said, "I'm drunk, but I'm not THAT drunk. I'm not weak minded." That's all he needed to say in order to get his point across to the choreographer that the mind games needed to end. We share this story with you in order to let you know that you really need to be mindful of who you party with. Even if they can help your career, some people consider you nothing more than amusement. So, keep on the watch and be true to yourself!

We never did drugs, but we were around those that did (and there are lots of these people in this business). It's an art to be able to hang out with people who do recreational drugs while not partaking. While they were smoking, snorting, or injecting, we were sipping on an alcoholic beverage. The users were none the wiser. All they remembered was, as they were getting high, we were in the room. They connected us with them, and come audition time, guess who booked the job? We're going to be honest with you: this doesn't always work. In some cases, you may get labeled as a prude for not indulging. However, if you are like us and decide not to do drugs, this may be your best option, since many in Hollywood do indulge.

One last area we want to discuss is the agency-only job. You go to an audition and you're the most talented person in the room. You may destroy the audition while in the final group of dancers at the end of a long day of auditioning, and still you may not book the job. You wait for the call. No answer. You call your agent, they don't know anything. A month goes by, and you see the job you auditioned for on television. You wonder whatever happened. You watch to see which dancers made the cut. To your surprise, you notice that half of the people on stage dancing next to the artist were not even at the audition.

How could that be? Was there another audition? A secret callback? Nope. You've just been the victim of an agency-only job. This is where an agency offers reduced rates if the production company only uses their dancers! Typically, this works if the choreographer is also with the same agency.

If you fall victim to this situation, don't be disturbed. You now understand that for some jobs it may exist. Look at the audition as an opportunity to potentially change the mind of the choreographer the next time around. Remember, there is always another audition right around the corner.

CHAPTER TWELVE

STILL WANNA DANCE?

*W*e know that some of the topics and content in this book will be perceived as controversial. We respect the rights and privacy of our friends and acquaintances depicted in each story and situation we pose. Because we do respect their privacy, we purposely left off the names of the people involved.

What is more important than the people, are the lessons learned from each experience depicted in this book.

Becoming a successful dancer takes more than your ability. It takes the looks of a movie star, the savvy of a politician, and the smarts of a business person. We authored this book so that you could apply the lessons learned and not repeat our mistakes. Remember that you need to be an active participant in your career. Your agent does a small portion of the work. Your success or failure is completely in your hands.

If after reading this book, you decide this is the business for you, we have a short list of to do's to get you going:

➢ **Take a second to reflect on what you want out of the business and set a goal.** Do you want to dance in movies, music videos, or commercials? Do you want to use dance as an opportunity to sing, act, direct, or choreograph? Have some idea of what you want out of this business *before* you begin.

➢ **Set small but specific goals which will lead you to your ultimate goal.** The definition of insanity is doing the same thing and expecting a different result. Don't be like many dancers who stop working after they get an agent. By setting realistic small goals, you are actively measuring your success. Along the way, you may have to add or subtract to your goals, but keeping them small will make it much easier to succeed. For example, your goal could be to get a dance agent. Some small goals could be, call each agency found in this book and find out their audition dates and times. Another small goal could be to take dance class at one of the large dance studios in Los Angeles in order to network and improve your skills. The point is this:

BE ACTIVE!

> **Figure out what your look is.** This means experimenting with hair, clothing, and make up. Take practice photos with your camera phone so that you have an idea of what looks you can pull off.
> **Be around the business.** Take as many classes in Los Angeles as you can with the choreographers and dancers who are active in the business. This means going to The Edge and the Millennium Dance Complex. Develop a relationship with some of the other dancers, but especially get to know the choreographer. You could do this by taking class from them. After knowing them on a first name bases, offer to take them to lunch and pick their brain.

These are just a few ideas we have done in order to establish relationships and succeed in the business. It's all about your look and who you know, so investing time in these things will pay off in the end.

There are five dance agencies with at least 300 professional dancers on roster each. That's 1500 dancers. Only about 5% - 10% work every week. The vast majority attends audition after audition and never gets a sniff at a job. A big reason why is because they don't *do* anything. They are not *active* in their career. You now have the knowledge to succeed. It's up to you to apply what you learn.

-        Now get out there and LEAN | BOOK | SUCCEED!

Index